D1444301

Gallery Books
Editor: Peter Fallon

LIVING QUARTERS

Brian Friel

LIVING QUARTERS

after Hippolytus

Gallery Books

This edition of
Living Quarters
is first published
simultaneously in paperback
and in a clothbound edition
in April 1992.

The Gallery Press
Loughcrew
Oldcastle
County Meath
Ireland

ISBN 1 85235 090 3 (*paperback*)
  1 85235 091 1 (*clothbound*)

Living Quarters was published first by Faber and Faber Limited in 1978. All rights whatsoever in this play are strictly reserved. Requests to reproduce the text in whole or in part should be addressed to the publishers. Application for performance in any medium or for translation into any language should be addressed to the author's sole agent Curtis Brown Group Ltd., 162-168 Regent Street, London W1R 5TB.

 The Gallery Press receives financial assistance from An Chomhairle Ealaíon / The Arts Council, Ireland, and acknowledges also the assistance of the Arts Council of Northern Ireland in the publication of this book.

Characters

SIR
COMMANDANT FRANK BUTLER
HELEN KELLY
MIRIAM DONNELLY
BEN
TINA
FATHER TOM CARTY
CHARLIE DONNELLY
ANNA

SIR: Middle-aged. Always in full control of the situation, of the other characters, of himself. His calm is never ruffled. He is endlessly patient and tolerant, but never superior. Always carries his ledger with him. Dressed in a dark lounge suit, dark tie, white shirt, black, highly polished shoes.

COMMANDANT FRANK BUTLER: Tall, lean, military man in his early fifties. Grey hair, military moustache. Has been in the Irish army all his life.

Four children by his first marriage:

HELEN KELLY: Twenty-seven, divorced; has been living in London for six year. An attractive woman with style and apparent self-assurance.

MIRIAM DONNELLY: Twenty-five, married to Charlie Donnelly; mother of three children. Plump, practical. Chain-smokes.

BEN: Twenty-four, hesitant, nervous, with a volatile face. Miriam describes him as a 'mother's boy'.

TINA: Eighteen, the youngest, 'the pet of the family', fresh, warm, eager.

FATHER TOM CARTY: Sixty-four, chaplain to the camp, with the rank of Commandant. A self-aware man with a professional, breezy manner. (Preferably overweight.)

CHARLIE DONNELLY: Early thirties; Miriam's husband; court clerk; cautious and proper; always with a raincoat across his arm. Views the Butler family with smiling caution.

ANNA: Early twenties; Frank's second wife; mature, intelligent, passionate, direct in speech and manner.

Time and place

The present in Ireland.

Set

Commandant Frank Butler's living quarters — a detached house close to a small military barracks in a remote part of County Donegal, Ireland.

The action takes place in the living-room and garden on a warm May evening and night. The living-room and garden have acting areas of almost equal size (left and right from the point of view of the audience).

The furnishings of the living-room are old and worn. Fireplace in the centre; an armchair on each side. The armchair left of the fireplace is of wicker. Small table, television set, sideboard on which are drinks. Some family photographs on the walls. On the mantelpiece a distinctive glass ornament with pendulous glass lobes. Door left of the fireplace leads to the kitchen off. Door right of the fireplace (used once in Act Two). A third door right leads to the hallway, which we see. Hallstand, small table, etc. A stairway rises from the hall. Another door (invisible and approximately opposite the fireplace) in the fourth, invisible, wall separating the living-room from the garden.

The garden begins at the front door and runs the full length of the side of the house, i.e. right across the front of the stage. In the garden a summer seat and some old deck chairs.

Down left, tucked into the corner, is a small, low footstool used only by Sir.

Living Quarters was first produced by The Abbey Theatre, Dublin, on 24 March 1977. The cast was as follows:

SIR	Clive Geraghty
COMMANDANT FRANK BUTLER	Ray McAnally
HELEN KELLY	Fedelma Cullen
MIRIAM DONNELLY	Maire Hastings
BEN	Stephen Brennan
TINA	Bernadette Shortt
FATHER TOM CARTY	Michael O'hAonghusa
CHARLIE DONNELLY	Niall O'Brien
ANNA	Dearbhla Molloy

Direction   Joe Dowling

for Seamus Deane

ACT ONE

SIR *sits on his stool down left, his ledger closed on his knee. Nobody else on stage.*

SIR The home, the house, the living quarters of Commandant Frank Butler, OC of B Company of the 37th Battalion of the Permanent Defence Forces. It is here on May 24th some years ago that our story is set, as they say — as if it were a feast laid out for consumption or a trap waiting to spring. And the people who were involved in the events of that day, although they're now scattered all over the world, every so often in sudden moments of privacy, of isolation, of panic, they remember that day, and in their imagination they reconvene here to reconstruct it — what was said, what was not said, what was done, what was not done, what might have been said, what might have been done; endlessly raking over those dead episodes that can't be left at peace.

He rises and moves to centre stage.

But reverie alone isn't adequate for them. And in their imagination, out of some deep psychic necessity, they have conceived this *(ledger)* — a complete and detailed record of everything that was said and done that day, as if its very existence must afford them their justification, as if in some tiny, forgotten detail buried here — a smile, a hesitation, a tentative gesture — if only it could be found and recalled — in it must lie the key to an understanding of *all* that happened. And in their imagination, out of some deep psychic necessity,

11

they have conceived me — the ultimate arbiter, the powerful and impartial referee, the final adjudicator, a kind of human Hansard who knows those tiny little details and interprets them accurately. And yet no sooner do they conceive me with my authority and my knowledge than they begin flirting with the idea of circumventing me, of foxing me, of outwitting me. Curious, isn't it? But to get back to that day.

He moves into the living-room, which now lights up.

May 24th; Commandant Frank Butler's home just outside the village of Ballybeg; a remote and run-down army camp in the wilds of County Donegal; and a day of celebration because Commandant Butler and his company have returned in triumph after five months service with the United Nations in the Middle East. And their return is triumphant because in their last week of duty, at an outpost called Hari, *(Reads)* 'while under siege and heavily outnumbered by guerrillas they responded gallantly, Commandant Butler behaving with outstanding courage and self-lessness, personally exposing himself to heavy and persistent fire to carry nine of his wounded men to safety'. And this evening top army brass and politicians and local dignitaries have gathered here to celebrate the triumphant return and to honour the triumphant Commandant. So much for the occasion. And hovering in the wings, once more reconvened in recollection to take yet another look at the events of that day, is the Butler family.

He now moves around the living-room and addresses the family off.

Are we all set? Good. Now — you've all been over this hundreds, thousands of times before. So on this occasion — with your co-operation, of course — what I would like to do is organize those recollections for you, impose a structure on them, just to give them a form of sorts. Agreed? Excellent! Naturally we'll only get through a tiny portion of all that was said and done that day; but I think we should attempt some kind of chronological order; and I promise you that the selection I make will be as fair and as representative as possible. So I'll call you as I require you and introduce you then. Agreed? Fine! (*Opens ledger*) Let's see. 'Helen arrives' — we'll not go back as far as that. 'Anna takes up her dress skirt. Tina prepares lunch' — we can skip all that. Yes — let's begin here: 'It is late afternoon. Anna is in bed. Tina is sponging her father's dress suit. In the camp Frank Butler is greeting his distinguished guests. Helen is out for a walk. Miriam has gone to the mess for a carton of ice cream. Ben is washing a shirt in his caravan in the sand dunes.' So. We require only Tina at the moment. And remember — it's all here, every single syllable of it. But if you wish to speak your thoughts as well — by all means. Thank you. Thank you.

SIR *looks around the set and goes to adjust the position of the garden seat.* TOM *enters.*

TOM Sir.

SIR (*Busy*) What is it, Father?

TOM I don't suppose it would be a breach of secrecy or etiquette if I — if you were to let me know how I'm described there, would it? You know — something to hang the cap on — 'good guy', 'funny guy', 'bit of a gossip'. Which of my many fascinating personas should I portray?

SIR (*Still busy*) You'll be yourself, Father.

TOM Of course. Naturally. But you've a description there, haven't you? And an objective view would be a help.

SIR I don't think so.

TOM As chaplain I've a right to — (*Pleasant again*) Please.

SIR I think you shouldn't.

TOM Please.

SIR *regards him calmly.*

SIR Very well.

TOM (*Breezily*) Soldier — man of God — friend of the boys — you name it.

SIR 'Father Thomas Carty, sixty-four years of age, chaplain, Commandant, close friend of the Butler family.'

TOM (*Saluting*) Yours truly.

ANNA *enters in her dressing-gown. She stands at a distance and watches this scene.*

SIR 'Married Frank and Louise — '

TOM May the Lord have mercy on her.

SIR ' — baptized their children and grandchildren: and six months ago married Frank again — to Anna.'

TOM Indeed. A happy day.

SIR 'The children used to call him Uncle — Uncle Tom — '

TOM (*Delighted*) Tina still does — occasionally.

SIR '"Is Uncle Tom coming with us?" they'd say. And he did. Always. Everywhere. Himself and the batman — in attendance.'

TOM That's one way of —

SIR ' — and that pathetic dependence on the Butler family, together with his excessive drinking make him a cliché, a stereotype. He knows this himself — '

TOM Cliché? For God's sake — !

SIR ' — but he is not a fool. He recognizes that this definition allows him to be witness to their pain but absolves him from experiencing it; appoints him confidant but acquits him of the responsibility of conscience — '

TOM That's not how — ! Oh my God . . .

SIR 'As the tale unfolds they may go to him for advice, not because they respect him, consider him wise — '

TOM (*Sudden revolt*) Because they love me, that's why! They love me!

SIR ' — but because he is the outsider who represents the society they'll begin to feel alienated from, slipping away from them.'

TOM (*Beaten*) Outsider?

ANNA *goes to* TOM *and puts her arm around him.*

SIR 'And what he says won't make the slightest difference because at that point — the point of no return — they'll be past listening to anybody. At that point all they'll hear is their own persistent inner voices — ' And so on and so forth.

TOM (*On point of tears*) Oh my God — Oh my God —

SIR It's your role.

TOM No, it's not. No, no, no, it's not.

SIR And to have any role is always something.

ANNA *begins to lead* TOM *away.*

When you've thought about it, you'll agree with me.

TOM No, no, no —

SIR And you'll do it.

TOM No, no —

SIR Oh, yes, you'll do it. Now I think everything's in position.

CHARLIE *enters. Almost furtive. Almost ingratiating.*

CHARLIE By the way, Sir —

SIR You're not needed, Charlie.

CHARLIE Because I'm not one of the family?

SIR Because we're beginning in the afternoon.

CHARLIE But I *was* there that night, you know, and —

SIR Early afternoon, Charlie.

CHARLIE But I *did* come — about half-eleven — to pick up Miriam.

SIR I know.

CHARLIE And I would have been here earlier, only I had to leave the baby-sitter home.

SIR I know.

CHARLIE And if I'm nervous, she's late — I mean to say, if I'm late, she's nervous.

SIR I know.

CHARLIE But I did get here before midnight. And doesn't that make me a witness? Relevant material, as we say.

SIR Charlie, if I need you, I'll call you.

CHARLIE Tell you what: supposing I just sat about, you know, and looked on, I'd —

SIR There are no spectators, Charlie. Only participants.

CHARLIE Promise you — wouldn't open my mouth —

SIR If your turn comes, I'll call you.

CHARLIE Could keep an eye on the ledger for you.

SIR Charlie.

CHARLIE Oh, well — see you later — good luck.

He leaves.

SIR And now to begin. The Butler home. Early evening of May 24th.

He sits on his low stool. Lights change. TINA enters from kitchen. The jacket of her father's dress suit is lying across an ironing-board and she is carrying a bowl of water to clean stains. We can hear in the far distance a military band playing. TINA listens to the music for a few seconds and then hums the melody.

'Tina, the youngest of the four Butler children. The pet of the family. Singing because her father is back from the Middle East and because she has never seen such excitement in the camp before. Her life up to this has been protected and generally happy and content. True, her mother died. But that was six years ago. And Tina loves her stepmother, Anna, at least as much as she loved her mother.'

HELEN enters left and crosses slowly to the garden seat right. She is carrying a bunch of May flowers. As she passes the living-room TINA sees her. She calls out.

TINA Helen!

HELEN Hello.

TINA It's like a carnival, isn't it?

HELEN Yes.

TINA The Number One Army Band — first time ever in

Ballybeg!
HELEN I know.
TINA Did you have a swim?
HELEN What?
TINA Did you swim?
HELEN Paddled.
TINA Oh, you're daring!
HELEN I am.
TINA Was it cold?
HELEN Can't hear you. Come on out — it's glorious.
TINA When I finish this.

HELEN *places the flowers on the seat and picks up the broken ones.* TINA *exits to the kitchen.*

SIR 'The eldest of the family — Helen. Twenty-seven and divorced. When she was nineteen and impetuous and strong-willed, she married Private Gerry Kelly, her father's batman, despite her mother's bitter and vicious opposition. The marriage lasted a few months. Private Kelly deserted and vanished. And Helen went to London. This is only her second time home since then. The last time was for her mother's funeral.'

HELEN *stands still.*

HELEN When I got off the bus and walked in there this morning the room was still stifling with her invalid's smell. Strange, wasn't it? And small things I thought I'd forgotten: her tiny, perfect, white teeth; the skin smooth and shiny over the arthritic knuckles; her walking-stick hooked on the back of the wicker chair. And that glass ornament on the mantelpiece that trembled when she screamed at me — (*Calmly, flatly*) 'You can't marry him, you little vixen! *Noblesse oblige!* D'you hear — *noblesse oblige!*'
SIR She never spoke to you again?
HELEN No.
SIR Nor to him?
HELEN Never to him.

SIR Do you still feel anger?

HELEN No, not a bit, I think. Not a bit.

SIR And him — how real is he?

HELEN Gerry? That's over.

SIR Altogether?

HELEN I'm wary. I'm controlled. I discipline myself.

SIR Then this homecoming was a risk?

HELEN In a way.

SIR A test? A deliberate test?

HELEN Perhaps.

SIR And you're surviving it?

HELEN I'm surviving it.

SIR All right, Helen, you've tested yourself and you've paid your respects to your father. You could leave now.

HELEN No. I'll see it through.

SIR Your discipline may not hold.

HELEN How can I be sure that I want it to?

SIR Only you can answer that.

> *She suddenly busies herself with the flowers.* MIRIAM *comes briskly through the front door, the hall, into the living-room.*

MIRIAM Oh my God — that heat!

> *Once in the living-room* MIRIAM *gets three plates from the sideboard and begins dividing the carton of ice cream she has brought home.*

SIR 'Miriam — the middle daughter. Married to Charlie Donnelly, clerk of the district court. She has three children. She is thinking of them.'

MIRIAM They should be arriving home from school just about now. I hope they don't feel altogether abandoned.

SIR She hasn't seen them for three hours.

MIRIAM I gave them soup and sandwiches and a bar of chocolate each for lunch; and Mrs Moyne'll have a hot meal ready for them when they get back. And she'll stay with them until Charlie gets home from the court in

Glenties. Then he'll leave her home and come back and make them liver and bacon for their tea. And then he'll go and collect her again and she'll get them porridge and bread and jam for supper and put them to bed.

SIR They are not neglected children.

MIRIAM Then he'll come and collect me and we should be home soon after midnight. He doesn't like hanging about here — no more than I do myself.

SIR 'Before she married, Miriam was a nurse.'

MIRIAM All the same it's a big day for Papa and I'm glad I came. God, wouldn't the kids love some of this ice cream!

SIR *looks at the audience and spreads his hands.*

(*Calling*) Who's for ice cream? Anyone for ice cream?

TINA (*From kitchen*) Me!

MIRIAM *carries the tray of dishes out to the garden.*

MIRIAM Ice cream, Helen?

HELEN Lovely.

MIRIAM Did you ever see the likes of that crowd milling about the gates?

HELEN I came up the back way.

MIRIAM TV cameras and reporters and what-not. And Sergeant Burke trying to control the traffic and looking as if he was going to cry. And that mad wife of his with her hair dyed a bright orange, beside herself with excitement and blowing kisses into all the nobs' cars as they pass through the gate. Sweet God — bedlam! And all the buckos from the village — the Morans and the Sharkeys and all that gang — all squinting and gleeking and not missing a bar. Oh, but there'll be tales to be told for years to come.

TINA *has joined them.*

TINA (*To* MIRIAM) Did you get the May flowers?

MIRIAM Not me — her ladyship here.

HELEN   Aren't they pretty?

TINA   Remember — we used to gather great armfuls of them and put them up on the May altar on the landing.

MIRIAM   In jam jars. (*Passes plate*) Here.

TINA   And bundles of bluebells that would go limp overnight and hang over the sides.

HELEN   The smell of them through the house — a sickly smell, wasn't it?

TINA   And us kneeling on the lino for the prayers and easing up one knee and then the other with the pain. Do you remember, Helen?

Very brief pause.

HELEN   That meadow beyond the school's full of flowers.

MIRIAM   What meadow's that?

TINA   Phil the Butcher's field.

HELEN   Phil Boyle and Mary! I saw him watching me from behind the byre, but I couldn't remember his name.

MIRIAM   Baldy Phil and Hairy Mary — I never could enjoy meat from that place.

TINA   Did you not speak to him?

HELEN   No, he wouldn't remember me now.

TINA   'Course he would.

MIRIAM   God, they must be ancient, that pair.

TINA   D'you remember — Mammy used to send us for eggs every Saturday morning —

MIRIAM   'You're to say: "A dozen eggs for *Commandant* Butler, please"' — hoping to get them cheap!

TINA   And if Ben came with us, Mary'd always give him a huge kiss.

MIRIAM   A rub of her beard!

TINA   And he always cried and then she'd give him a duck egg for himself and Daddy used to say he cried just to get the duck egg — d'you remember?

MIRIAM   Oh, sweet God!

TINA   D'you remember, Helen?

As HELEN *passes her she hugs her briefly. Pause.*

HELEN   Yes. Yes, I remember.

MIRIAM God bless Mammy and make her healthy again. God bless Daddy and have him transferred to Dublin.

TINA   We all had that bit.

MIRIAM God bless Uncle Tom and make him a good priest. God bless Helen, Ben and Tina. And God bless me and give me bigger thighs than Josie McGrenra. And I got them.

TINA   What's this my rhyme was? God bless Mammy, Daddy, Uncle Tom, Helen, Miriam, Ben and Stinky Bum Blue.

MIRIAM Who?

TINA   A rag doll. Still have her. God bless the Irish army and make it strong and brave.

MIRIAM *and* HELEN *laugh.*

HELEN   Tina!

TINA   That's true. And look at Daddy! And God bless me and take me up to heaven before my tenth birthday.

MIRIAM Weren't you lucky you were ignored!

HELEN ⎱ Does he come — ?
TINA ⎰ What did you — ?

TINA   Sorry — go ahead.

HELEN   I was just going to ask you, do you see Ben often?

TINA   You know Ben.

MIRIAM Yes!

TINA   Whenever he takes the notion. When Daddy was out in the Middle East he called in maybe a couple of times a week. But now that he's back —

MIRIAM Did you know that Charlie got him a job driving the mobile library? Surely to God that wasn't too taxing on him. And he stuck it for how long? Four days. Walked out without as much as a by your leave. Left the bloody library van sitting out in the bogs beyond Loughcrillan. Oh, that fella!

HELEN   Do they speak at all?

TINA   Daddy and him? When they meet. If they have to.

HELEN   I thought I might have run into him when I was down at the shore. Where has he got his caravan?

TINA   God knows where you'd find him. Sometimes he

works on the boats. Or does odd days labouring. And
then he disappears for weeks — I don't know where
he goes — Scotland — Dublin. But he always comes
back. Always.

MIRIAM Like malaria.

TINA But if he's around and hears you're here he'll be sure
to call.

HELEN I hope so.

MIRIAM Listen to me — let there be no romantic aul' chat about
brother Ben. He's a wastrel — a spoiled mother's boy.
And if he turns up today to ruin the biggest event in
Father's life I'll soon send him packing. So. (*Lights a
cigarette*) Sure you're not smoking?

HELEN Positive.

TINA Three years off — isn't she great?

MIRIAM Magnificent. Tell us about London.

HELEN It's all right. The same office job, the same landlady
since I went there.

MIRIAM Digs or flat?

HELEN Digs.

TINA Mrs Zimmermann from Zürich.

HELEN If she thinks I need cheering up she says: 'Come and
have a cup of coffee with me, Mrs Kelly. I have a most
funny joke to impart to you.'

MIRIAM (*Finishing ice cream*) That was good. Does she feed you
well?

HELEN Very well.

TINA And her four cats and her seventeen canaries and her
son, a medical student.

MIRIAM How do you know all that?

TINA We write occasionally.

MIRIAM If the Donnellys get a card at Christmas they feel
honoured.

HELEN We're finished with cats and canaries and we're into
Pekinese dogs now. And the son's a successful young
doctor —

TINA Jean.

MIRIAM Jean — with a large practice. And the confidential
stories she insists on telling me about him and his
private life and his patients — I can't stop her.

TINA Is he handsome?

HELEN In a way.

MIRIAM Well?

HELEN And married.

MIRIAM Bugger him — that's him scrubbed. Oh, isn't that just perfect.

> TINA *and* MIRIAM *stretch out in the sun.* HELEN *sits upright.*

TINA It's almost too hot for me.

MIRIAM Don't know when I sunbathed last.

TINA Glorious.

MIRIAM We'll come out in blisters.

TINA Yes, nurse.

MIRIAM Any olive oil in the house?

TINA Kitchen.

MIRIAM Where?

TINA Bottom press.

MIRIAM I suppose you wouldn't go for it?

TINA Too lazy.

MIRIAM Me, too. God, the big snout'll be like a beacon. (TINA *laughs*) We get one hot day every five years and it goes to our heads. Oh, perfect — perfect —

> HELEN *looks at them for a few seconds. Then, very suddenly, she goes down to* SIR. *Addresses him in urgent undertones.*

HELEN It's not right! It's not right!

SIR Yes, it is.

HELEN No, it's not. It's distorted — inaccurate.

SIR I would tell you. Trust me.

HELEN The whole atmosphere — three sisters, relaxed, happy, chatting in their father's garden on a sunny afternoon. There was unease — I *remember* — there were shadows — we've got to acknowledge them!

SIR Why?

HELEN Because they were part of it.

SIR Don't you think they're aware of them? They're thinking the very same thing themselves. (HELEN *looks up at her sisters*) Believe me — it's exactly right. (*Pause*) Go on — join them again.

HELEN *goes back. Stands looking at them.*

TINA (*Her eyes closed*) Do you have to go back tomorrow?

HELEN Afraid so.

TINA Hardly worth your while for one night, was it?

HELEN I've paid my respects to the Commandant.

TINA When you phoned you were coming he was really thrilled.

HELEN And I saw you two, didn't I?

MIRIAM A sight that has driven strong men to distraction. (*She sits up*) God, that's too much for me. And you met our new stepmother.

TINA (*Sitting up*) And she liked her — didn't you, Helen? So there!

MIRIAM So what?

TINA So she thinks she's beautiful — that's what. And so do I.

MIRIAM All I ever said —

HELEN Shhh!

MIRIAM Damn the hair I care if she hears me or not. I just think she's far too young for him and that the quiet of this backwater'll drive her bonkers. You and her and a batman running this house — I mean what the hell do you *do* all day?

TINA She loves Ballybeg — she told me.

MIRIAM As for himself, you'd hardly describe him as a court jester, would you? I mean he's set in his ways and damned selfish and bossy and —

TINA Selfish? After the way he nursed Mammy for years?

MIRIAM So well he might.

TINA What does that mean?

HELEN Will you both keep your voices down!

TINA (*To* HELEN) What does she mean by that?

MIRIAM That this bloody wet hole ruined her health and that he wouldn't accept a transfer — always waiting for the big promotion that would be worthy of him and that never came. Clonmel, Templemore, Mullingar, Kilkenny — they all came up at different times and he wangled his way out of them — not important enough for Commandant Butler. Well, he'll probably get what he wants as a result of this ballyhoo and I wish him luck — I really do — himself and his child bride. I'd strip in a minute, only those Sharkey stallions would be sure to be peeping over that hedge.

TINA What any of us thinks isn't important. What is important is that he loves her and she loves him.

MIRIAM Mother of God! Would you grow up, child.

TINA And they're perfectly happy together.

MIRIAM Married for five months and out of that they've been together all of what? — ten days?

TINA Amn't I right, Helen?

MIRIAM Unless the daily love letters count — do they?

TINA Amn't I right, Helen?

MIRIAM How would she know? She's a stranger here.

Suddenly sorry, she jumps up and kisses HELEN.

Sorry, sorry sweetie — I didn't mean that. Really. I'm a coarse bitch. Always was. You know that. Sorry. (*She sits down again*) As mother used to say — (*Grand accent*) 'Miriam, you're neither a Butler nor a Hogan. I'm afraid you're just — pure Ballybeg.' (HELEN *and* TINA *laugh.* MIRIAM *closes eyes again*) Not a day passes but I thank God for that eejit, Charlie Donnelly. (*Military music in the distance — the same piece as before*) She always called him 'Charles'. But I think she liked him.

TINA Of course she did.

MIRIAM But how could she? Maybe because his Uncle Mickey was land steward to the Duke of Abercorn.

They listen to the music. MIRIAM *hums with it.*

TINA I suppose you never hear from your Gerald, Helen?

HELEN 'My' Gerald?

TINA Gerald, then.

HELEN No.

MIRIAM *sits up.*

MIRIAM I hope to God the kids have the sense to have on their sun hats.

TINA And no idea where he is?

HELEN None.

HELEN *rises and gathers her flowers.*

MIRIAM Wouldn't you think that aul' band would have a second tune!

TINA Daddy said someone saw him recently in Liverpool.

HELEN Really.

MIRIAM Should be called the Only One Army Band.

TINA Whoever it was said he had a beard.

HELEN They go so limp in the sun, don't they?

TINA Do you ever think of him at all, Helen?

HELEN *passes* TINA *on her way into the living-room; as before, she hugs her briefly, only this time almost shaking her. As she hugs her:*

HELEN For God's sake, Tina darling, will you —

MIRIAM Oh, smart, smart, smart!

TINA I thought she might like to —

MIRIAM You thought! (*Calmer*) Come on — we'd better get Pop's duds laid out for him.

She sings the military music loudly as she gathers the plates. She and TINA *go into the living-room.* HELEN *is putting the flowers in water.*

Be marvellous, wouldn't it, if you turned a nice golden colour like those women in the travel brochures? God, aul' Charlie'd go off the head altogether! (*To* TINA) Are his black shoes ready?

TINA Not yet.

MIRIAM I'll do them and you do the suit — okay? (*To* HELEN) The years may have passed but we're still Daddy's little beavers!

TINA (*To* HELEN — *in apology*) Helen, I — I'm —

MIRIAM (*Catching her arm*) Get me the shoe polish, duckie, will you? You keep changing where you keep things in this damned house.

> MIRIAM *polishes the shoes.* TINA *presses the suit.* HELEN *goes out to the garden.* FRANK *enters by the front door. Dressed in commandant's UN uniform. Carrying two bottles. He pauses in the hall, looks up the stairs, calls gently.*

FRANK Anna?

SIR 'Commandant Frank Butler.'

FRANK Anna?

SIR 'Twelve months ago a widower, commandant of a remote barracks, surrendering hope. Today a young wife, the Hero of Hari, and certain promotion.' (*To* FRANK) 'Outstanding courage and selflessness' — is that accurate?

> FRANK *shrugs.*

SIR You're nervous.

FRANK Yes.

SIR Of what?

FRANK I don't know.

SIR Can it be to do with Anna?

FRANK Yes. Maybe. I don't know. With myself. I'm jittery for some reason.

SIR That's understandable.

FRANK And unhappy. Suddenly unhappy. Profoundly unhappy.

SIR It's the tension.

FRANK Yes?

SIR And all the fuss. All those people.

FRANK I suppose so.

SIR But remember — they're here to honour you.

FRANK I know that.

SIR So keep calm. Keep cool.

FRANK Yes.

SIR Everything's running smoothly. Everything's in hand.
FRANK Yes, yes. Everything's in hand.

He goes quickly into the living-room.

Anna must be asleep. We'll give her another quarter of an hour — it's going to be a tiring evening for her. (*Hands the bottles to* TINA) These are for later, in case we have some people back. Leave them on the sideboard. Did the cuff links turn up?
TINA In the jacket pocket.
FRANK I thought you said you looked there. (*To* MIRIAM) Are those ready?
MIRIAM Another minute, Commandant, sir.
FRANK (*To* TINA) And Anna's stuff — her dress and all that — that's all arranged?
TINA Lying on the bed in Ben's old room. Everything's perfect. Stop fussing, Daddy.
FRANK No, I'll tell you what you can do: give her another ten minutes and then bring her a cup of tea.
TINA What about yourself?
FRANK I think I'll take a drink instead — no, maybe I shouldn't. Yes, I'll take a cup of tea, too.
MIRIAM What are they all at over there?
FRANK Standing around, talking, drinking.
MIRIAM Isn't it time you changed?
FRANK I know. And I've still to get a speech ready.
TINA Helen'll help you.
MIRIAM (*Offering the shoes*) There you are.
FRANK I don't want them just now, do I?

MIRIAM *makes a face.*

(*To* TINA) Where is Helen?
TINA In the garden. (*Calls*) Helen! Daddy wants — !
FRANK Shhh — Anna. I can go out, can't I?

He goes out to the garden. MIRIAM *looks up at the ceiling.*

28

MIRIAM God, isn't he a charmer! Sooner you nor me, daughter.

> MIRIAM *goes into the kitchen. After a time* TINA *joins her.*

HELEN See the conquering hero comes;
   Sound the trumpets, beat the drums.
FRANK Hah!
HELEN (*Offering a flower*) For the Hero of Hari.
FRANK Thank you.

> *As he accepts it he leans over her as if he is about to kiss her forehead, hesitates, then quickly:*

Did you see the heading in today's *Donegal Enquirer*?
HELEN No.
FRANK It's above the photograph taken at the airport yesterday — 'President Greets Humble Hannibal.' (*They both laugh. He sits beside her*) God, I feel so ancient, Helen.
HELEN It'll soon be over.
FRANK Walking over here from the camp, d'you know what I was thinking: what has a lifetime in the army done to me? Wondering have I carried over into this life the too rigid military discipline that — that the domestic life must have been bruised, damaged, by the stern attitudes that are necessary in the — I suppose what I'm saying is that I'm not unaware of certain shortcomings in my relationships with your mother and with Ben; and indeed with you when you and Gerald decided to —
HELEN The past's over, Father. And forgotten.
FRANK That's true. Over and forgotten. (*Then briskly — to their mutual relief*) Any good at writing after-dinner speeches?
HELEN Expert. What kind?
FRANK Short and brilliant. And modest.
HELEN Let's see. 'Gentlemen, I want to welcome you most sincerely, and even more sincerely to congratulate you on finding your way here.'

FRANK Ah-ha!

HELEN 'I will not dwell on the modest part I played in the event which the world now calls the Siege of Hari — '

FRANK I certainly will.

HELEN ' — and which brought fame and honour not only to United Nations troops everywhere — '

FRANK But also —

HELEN ' — to this country and to our own illustrious army.'

FRANK Hear, hear; hear, hear.

HELEN 'As for my own paltry part — '

FRANK Silence! Silence!

HELEN ' — as I carried each of those nine men back to safety — '

FRANK ' — across those burning desert wastes — '

HELEN ' — my one sustaining thought was — '

FRANK (*Quickly*) Do you know what it was?

HELEN ' — that you'd make me Chief of Staff as from this moment.'

FRANK And why not?

HELEN There you are — nothing to it.

FRANK I knew you'd be good.

HELEN Pleasure.

Pause.

FRANK When's your flight tomorrow?

HELEN Eleven.

FRANK I'll get someone to drive you to Derry.

HELEN I enjoy the bus.

FRANK I'm delighted you came, Helen. And very, very grateful.

HELEN A big occasion. A national hero.

FRANK For a day.

HELEN And some time before I go you must tell me exactly what happened. All I know is what I've read in the papers.

FRANK I'll post you a copy of the reports I've got to make out for GHQ.

HELEN Will you?

FRANK Promise.

Again a silence. And as before he stretches across instinctively to catch her hand. She looks at him. A moment of embarrassment. He pats her hand briskly instead.

Well, at least they're seeing the place at its best.

HELEN That's true.

FRANK In weather like this you forget how grim it can be. When you heard about Anna and me —

HELEN Yes?

FRANK Were you hurt?

HELEN Why would I be hurt?

FRANK That I hadn't told you about it in advance.

HELEN No, not at all.

FRANK We told nobody. It was all very — at my time of day I thought — just Anna and myself, and Tom. I suppose I should have told Tina, being in the house and all, but I knew Tina wouldn't mind. And I was on the point of phoning you one night but we decided — I felt — it would be better to present you all with the *fait accompli*. Very impressive little ceremony it was, too; quiet, you know, simple; very — that little Franciscan church in Dublin — the one along the quay. Full of atmosphere; lovely. And we came straight back here intending to take a honeymoon later. And then, as you know, no sooner am I back than I'm off for five months. So in a way we still haven't had a honeymoon — you're sure you didn't mind?

HELEN Positive.

FRANK As soon as the fuss dies down we'll head off somewhere.

HELEN So you should.

FRANK France, maybe.

HELEN You deserve a holiday.

FRANK Or Italy. Somewhere. (*Pause*) Have you and she had a chance to talk yet?

HELEN For half an hour or so.

FRANK Oh, good, good — yes?

HELEN We had lunch together.

FRANK Yes?

31

HELEN   Then I set her hair for her.

FRANK   Yes?

HELEN   Haven't you seen it?

FRANK   (*Sudden rush*) Isn't she beautiful, Helen? Isn't she beautiful?

HELEN   Yes.

FRANK   Yes, and warm and open and refreshing. And so direct — so direct — so uncomplicated. Anything she thinks — whatever comes into her head — straight out — it must come straight out — just like that. So unlike us: measured, watching, circling one another, peeping out, shying back.

HELEN   Is that us?

FRANK   Oh, yes, that's us — you, me, your mother —

HELEN   Tina?

FRANK   Tina's special, you know that, Tina's a baby.

HELEN   Is she? And Miriam?

FRANK   All right — maybe not Miriam.

HELEN   And Ben?

FRANK   I know nothing about him. But my mascot — I call her my mascot. A good name for her, isn't it? — whatever she is, it's there before you. And from the moment I met her — and I can say this to you, Helen: you're the only person I could say this to without embarrassment . . . . There! You see! Typical! You're withdrawing!

HELEN   I'm not! — I'm not!

FRANK   Yes, you are. And now I'm embarrassed. It's a family —

HELEN   Go on. Say what you were going to say.

FRANK   I can't now.

HELEN   Say it, Father.

        Pause.

FRANK   (*Simply*) What I was going to say is that for the first time in my life I am profoundly happy. (*Pause*) And now you're thinking there's no fool like an old fool.

HELEN   No.

FRANK   (*Quickly*) Infinitely happier than I ever was with your mother. Is that a despicable thing to say? No, it's not.

32

It's the truth. During all those years of illness she was patient and courageous and admirable. And I responded to that as best I could. Despite what Ben thinks, I did my best. But it had all withered into duty, Helen. There was no joy — the joy had gone. And that's what Anna did — she restored joy to me — she animated me again. If I'm a hero today — whatever that silly word means — it is because of her.

HELEN I'm sure that's true, Father.

FRANK And nothing would give me more pleasure than to bestow some of that joy on you.

HELEN Me?

FRANK If I could.

HELEN Why me?

FRANK Because I have a superabundance and because I sense a melancholy about my first child.

TINA *enters living-room with tray.*

TINA (*Calls*) Tea, everybody!

FRANK If that's not too arrogant of me — is it? (*He looks at her. Pause*) And now you're convinced I'm an old fool, aren't you?

HELEN You keep looking for reassurance, hero.

FRANK (*Rising briskly*) Do I? — It must be — because I need it. God, look at the time — and I've still to get dressed.

FRANK *goes quickly into the living-room.* TINA *is about to bring a cup of tea upstairs.*

Did you wake her up yet?

TINA On my way.

FRANK Take the suit with you, too.

He sits and changes his shoes. TOM *enters the hall carrying a camera.*

TOM Hannibal!

FRANK I can see that's going to stick.

TOM (*Breezy, confident to* SIR) You were right — I'll do it.

33

SIR I knew you would.

TOM But maybe not as you think. You just can't label a man a cliché and write him off.

SIR The assessment isn't mine.

TOM Just watch and you'll see. You may be surprised.

SIR I'm watching.

TINA *goes into the hall.*

TOM Tina, my love, are they ready?

TINA Almost. You're looking great, Uncle Tom.

TOM Feeling terrific, thank the Lord, terrific.

TINA *goes upstairs.* TOM *goes into the living-room.* MIRIAM *enters from the kitchen.*

Is this all the length you are?

FRANK Aren't you dressing?

TOM I'm not one of the big shots. And how are you, Miriam?

MIRIAM Great, thanks, Father.

FRANK Are they getting restless over there?

TOM Just waiting breathlessly in the ante-room to get a glimpse of you.

FRANK Go to hell.

TOM (*To* MIRIAM) Hoping to touch his sleeve as he passes.

FRANK (*Leaving*) Give him a drink, Miriam.

TOM The way he said that you'd think my tongue was hanging out. Nothing for me, thanks.

MIRIAM It's a thirsty day.

TOM Honestly. How's Charlie?

MIRIAM Great.

TOM Pity you didn't bring the kids — they'd have enjoyed the band.

MIRIAM Isn't there chaos enough? Have you seen Helen yet?

TOM Where?

MIRIAM Here.

TOM She's not!

MIRIAM Arrived this morning.

TOM Well, good Lord! Why did nobody tell me?

He goes out to the garden.

I've only just heard.

HELEN Father Tom! It's good to see you!

He embraces her.

TOM It's great to see you, Helen. How *are* you? Show me —
you've lost weight.

HELEN I don't think so — have I?

TOM The answer I want is: as a matter of fact I have, Uncle
Tom, and so have you.

They both move into the living-room.

HELEN Well, as a matter of fact, Father —

TOM Don't tell me. I know. I know.

MIRIAM Looking powerful, isn't he?

HELEN You are.

TOM I'm grotesque. Food, drink and sloth — they're killing me. The question is: will I survive until next
November?

HELEN Why then?

TOM That's when I retire. And even if I last six months
more, what's to become of me then? Kicked out of the
only world I've known for forty years — I'll be lost.
D'you know who I met the other day? Jackie Sheridan
— Daddy knows him — chaplain down at Athlone all
his life. Retired last year; living with a widowed sister
in Waterford. And d'you know what he does to pass
the time? Studies all the death notices in the morning
paper and spends the rest of the day writing letters of
condolence to the relatives. Black strangers! Honestly.
Terrifying, isn't it? What d'you think of Anna?

HELEN That was always an old trick of yours.

TOM Trick? Trick? What trick?

HELEN The disarming chatter and then the sudden, probing
question.

MIRIAM She's wise to you, Father Tom.

TOM (*To* MIRIAM, *who is laughing*) Is that fair? D'you think that's fair? (*To* HELEN) Well, I think she's terrific. And sure the world knows Frank's terrific.

HELEN So they'll make a terrific couple.

TOM (*To* MIRIAM) Lord, hasn't she got sharp!

MIRIAM England smartens them up all right.

TOM I didn't mean that at all.

HELEN Yes, you did.

TOM Tell me, girls, I want your advice. The powers that be have some kind of a notion that on a night like this I always get plastered.

MIRIAM Tch-tch-tch.

TOM Wait — wait — wait! Now — should I confirm that notion for them? Or should I stay sober and confound them? I could, you know.

HELEN Confirm them?

TOM Confound them!

MIRIAM Do that then, Father.

TOM Should I?

MIRIAM Anything to confound them.

TOM That's it then. Settled. (*To* HELEN) What are you looking sceptical about?

HELEN Not a thing — not a thing.

> FRANK *enters in his dress uniform.* TINA *behind him.*

FRANK Anna'll be down in a minute.

> *The following lines* — MIRIAM's, TOM's, HELEN's, TINA's — *all overlap.*

MIRIAM (*Clapping*) Well — well — well — well!

TOM Ah, the prince himself!

HELEN Very smart — very smart indeed!

TINA Three cheers for the hero!

TOM (*Sings*) For he's a jolly good fellow —

FRANK Stop — stop — stop — stop — stop!

ALL } For he's a jolly good fellow;
TOGETHER } For he's a jolly good fellow;
And so say all of us.

TOM Everybody outside for a picture!

TINA A photo — hurrah — hurrah — hurrah — a photo!

They move to the garden — talking — still singing/ humming 'Jolly Good Fellow'. Comments like: 'My God, look at my dress', 'Anybody got a comb?', 'You're fine', 'Where do you want us to stand?' etc., etc.

TOM Over here, please, everybody. You in the middle, Frank. Miriam, you and Tina on one side.

FRANK Where? Here?

TOM A bit to the left.

FRANK Here?

TOM That's the right.

FRANK It's *my* left.

TOM No wonder you could never march!

TINA What about me?

TOM Fine where you are.

MIRIAM Not a word — the cap's still over the lens.

HELEN It's not!

TOM You're quite right — so it is! (*Takes it off*) That'll be a help.

MIRIAM Maybe — maybe.

TOM A little tighter in, Helen, please. Good, good. At ease, Frank.

FRANK I am at ease.

TOM Are you? Look at me. Big smile, everybody.

The group is facing almost straight out. ANNA *in a long dressing-gown comes downstairs and into the living-room. She looks around.*

ANNA (*Softly*) Frank?

She looks out, sees the photographing, stands watching.

TINA Cheese — isn't that what you say?

HELEN *Noblesse oblige.*

MIRIAM Oh, very posh. Is that a London one?

ANNA (*More loudly*) Frank!

FRANK Come on, Tom. Get a move on.

SIR 'She calls Frank twice. But Frank does not hear her. And she goes back to her room and cries.'

TOM Little tighter in, love.

TINA Me?

TOM No, Miriam. Tight in — perfect!

ANNA Look at them — tight — tight — tight — arms around one another — smiling. No, I won't go back to my room and cry. I'll tell them now!

SIR gets quickly to his feet and goes to ANNA.

SIR They won't hear you now.

ANNA They will! They will!

SIR Anna, believe me —

She rushes away from him and out to the garden where she stands facing the group. SIR looks on patiently. She is almost hysterical.

TOM Frank.

FRANK What?

TOM This way.

FRANK I'm glaring at you, for God's sake!

TOM That's what I'm saying. Will you stop it! Now — terrific — Commandant Butler and his beautiful family.

MIRIAM He really means me.

ANNA (*Trying to control herself*) Listen to me, all of you. You, too, Chaplain.

MIRIAM No film in the camera.

TINA I'm going to laugh.

ANNA When you were away, all those months I was left alone here —

TOM Great — don't move — terrific. And another.

ANNA Listen to me, Frank!

FRANK (*To* TOM) No, no, no, no.

TOM One more — just one more — that's all.

ANNA I had an affair with your son, Ben — with your brother, Ben! An affair — an affair — d'you hear!

TOM Even closer together.

MIRIAM Thanks be to God Charlie isn't watching this caper.

ANNA An affair, d'you hear — out of loneliness, out of despair, out of hate! And everybody in the camp knows — everybody except the Butlers!

> TINA *can control her laughter no longer — she explodes.*

TOM Terrific, Tina! Everybody join in!

> *The laughter is infectious. They laugh so much we can hardly hear what they are saying.*

MIRIAM *Noblesse oblige*!

TOM Lovely, Frank.

HELEN Is there really no film in it?

TINA Hold me up! Hold me up!

TOM (*Clicking, clicking*) Terrific, terrific! Stay where you are!

> ANNA *is staring at the others as if she had come out of a dream.* SIR *goes to her and takes her arm, leading her off.*

SIR I told you, didn't I? 'Frank does not hear her and she goes back to her room and cries.'

ANNA (*Crying*) It wasn't despair.

SIR I know.

ANNA And it wasn't hate — no, not hate for him.

SIR You'll tell us later.

ANNA It wasn't even loneliness —

SIR Later — later — you'll do it *later* exactly as it's here. Now go back to your room.

ANNA I'm sorry.

SIR No harm done.

ANNA Did I mess it all up?

SIR You shuffled the pages a bit — that's all. But nothing's changed.

Throughout this ANNA/SIR *exchange the others have stood with frozen smiles. Now that* ANNA *has gone off they are released again.*

TOM   There! Thank you — thank you — thank you.
FRANK Right — off we go, Tom. Let's move — let's move.

FRANK goes into the house and hall. The others drift into the living-room.

TOM   Can I leave this (*camera*) here?
TINA   I'll look after it.
HELEN   When will we get copies?
MIRIAM Have you never seen his pictures?
FRANK   (*Calling upstairs*) Anna! We're all set.
MIRIAM If you get a word with the Taoiseach, Father, tell him we're still waiting for the sewage out at Kilclooney.
TOM   The very first thing I'll say to him.
MIRIAM Just to give him an appetite.

ANNA comes downstairs. FRANK *stands at the bottom with his hands outstretched.*

FRANK   Beautiful.
ANNA   I'm nervous, Frank.
FRANK   You are beautiful. (*Calls*) Look! Everybody look! Look what I'm bringing to the reception!

The others move out to the hallway.

TOM   Terrific, Anna, terrific!
HELEN ⎫
MIRIAM ⎬ Lovely, Anna. It's a beautiful dress. You did the hair
TINA ⎭ very well. Those are lovely shoes. Lovely. Lovely.
FRANK   And look — look — (*jewellery*). And this, isn't this elegant (*dress*)?
ANNA   Frank, I —
FRANK   And what about that (*hair*)? Your handiwork, isn't it, Helen?
HELEN   You're going to be late, Father.

40

FRANK Let them wait.

ANNA Please, Frank.

FRANK All in all — beautiful!

ANNA Please —

FRANK And she says she's nervous! My darling, they'll never have seen a sight like it in the mess — in any mess — in all their puny lives. (*Briskly*) We're away. Don't wait up for me.

> BEN *enters left. Very diffident, very hesitant, as if he might turn and run away. He looks into the living-room — but the others have now moved out to the front of the house.*

TOM We're off. God bless.

HELEN Have a good time. Confound them, Father Tom.
MIRIAM Enjoy yourselves. Make a good speech, Daddy.
TINA Don't eat too much, Anna.

> *They are all offstage now — except* HELEN, *who is standing at the front door.*

FRANK Are we taking my car or yours?

TOM It doesn't matter — either.

TINA Take your own, Daddy.

> *The car moves off. We hear* TINA *and* MIRIAM *calling goodbyes.* HELEN *waves from the door.* BEN *moves closer to the house.* HELEN *turns and comes into the living-room.*

SIR 'Benedict Butler — Ben — twenty-four years of age. Only son of Frank and Louise. His father wanted him to go for a commission, but his mother wanted him to be a doctor. Was a first-year medical student at University College, Dublin, when his mother died.'

BEN (*Softly*) Helen.

> HELEN *is standing looking at the photographs on the mantelpiece. She has her back to him.*

41

SIR 'Shortly after her death his health broke down and he never went back to college. Now fully recovered; the only after-effect being a stammer which afflicts him occasionally when he is tense.'

BEN Helen.

SIR 'As he looks into the living-room he imagines for a second that the figure at the mantelpiece is his mother.'

BEN She had her back to me. She didn't hear me. And I stood outside in the garden and just watched her. Everything — her hair, her neck, her shoulders, the way she moved her arms — precisely as I remembered. (HELEN *is now fingering the glass ornament*) Not a sound except the tap-tap-tap of her stick as she moved about. And for a second my heart expanded with an immense remembered love for her, and then at once shrank in terror of her. And then suddenly she turned and came towards the open door, and I saw it wasn't — it w-w-w-wasn't —

HELEN has turned and has moved to the open door. She is startled to see a man staring in at her.

HELEN Who — ? (*Loud*) Ben!

He responds as if someone — a stranger — had called him.

BEN (*Quickly, confused*) Yes? Yes?

HELEN runs out and throws her arms around him.

HELEN ⎱ Oh — Ben, Ben, Ben, Ben, Ben!
BEN ⎰ Yes? Yes? Yes? Yes? Yes?

SIR (*Rising*) Thank you. (*Claps his hands twice to interrupt the action*) That's fine — that's fine. We're moving along very nicely. (*Sees that* BEN *and* HELEN *are still locked in an embrace*)

SIR Thank you.

They separate.

Yes, very nicely indeed.

As soon as he claps his hands, TINA, ANNA, FRANK *and* TOM *appear.*

Now, we'll leave it there, I think, and move straight on to the point when —

ANNA 'The point of no return'.

SIR The — ?

ANNA It's your phrase; you used it to Father Tom.

SIR 'The point of no return' — you're quite right; so I did. Wasn't that very histrionic of me! Oh, no; heavens, no. We're nowhere near that — that decisive point yet.

ANNA Then let's skip all the rest and go straight to it.

SIR You've already been naughty and attempted that, Anna!

ANNA Because it's the essence of it all, isn't it?

SIR Well, of course we can do that. But if we do, then we're bypassing all that period when different decisions *might* have been made. Because at the point we've arrived at now, many different conclusions would have been possible if certain things had been said or done or left unsaid and undone. And at this point it did occur to many of you to say certain things or to omit saying certain things. And it is the memory of those lost possibilities that has exercised you endlessly since and has kept bringing you back here, isn't that so?

TOM I'm sure he's right.

SIR For example, Helen, you did think of spending the night with Charlie and Miriam.

HELEN We've already been over all that.

SIR We have indeed. And what you said was, 'No, I'll see it through.' .

HELEN Yes, I stayed; and I saw it through; and I didn't survive the test. And I've cracked up three times since. Now are you content?

SIR It's your content we're talking about. And Ben, at this

point you still had time to join your friends on the salmon boat.

BEN Am I complaining? Am I?

SIR But the thought did occur to you. And they didn't set out for — what? — another hour at least. So if you would like to explore that area of —

BEN Just stick to the f-f-f-facts.

SIR But that is a fact. And every time you get drunk, it's the one thing you keep talking about.

BEN What happened happened. Leave it at that.

SIR As you wish. As for yourself, Anna, you could have resolved — sitting up at that top table in the mess — bored by the talk around you — you could still have resolved to live with your secret —

ANNA 'Live with my secret'! For God's sake!

SIR Be fair, Anna. You did think of it. In which case Frank's life would have stayed reasonably intact. Oh, there were many, many options still open at this stage.

TOM I agree completely. (*He is ignored*)

TINA For me, too?

SIR Not for you Tina, I'm afraid. You had no choice. That night you were faced with the inevitability of growing up. But that's all — well, almost all.

TOM He's absolutely right — about the rest of us, I mean. (*No one listens to him, either here or later when he preaches*)

SIR As for yourself, Frank —

FRANK *holds up his hands.*

FRANK You're in command, Sir.

SIR At this point, indeed at any point, you could well have —

FRANK Please — please. I did what I had to do. There was no alternative for me. None. What I had to do was absolutely clear-cut. There was never any doubt in my mind.

SIR I'm afraid that's true, Frank.

FRANK So carry on as you think best, Sir. I'm in your hands.

SIR Very well. Let's proceed. Let's leap ahead to — yes,

several hours later.

TOM Our options are still open — he's perfectly right.

SIR And for this episode I think I need only Helen and Ben and Tina.

TOM I'm not a sermonizing kind of fellow — good Lord, you know me better than that —

The others begin to drift away, each encased in his privacy.

— but I've got to speak what I know to be true, and that is that grace is available to each and every one of us if we just ask God for it —

SIR Yes — here we are.

TOM — which is really the Christian way of saying that our options are *always* open. Because that is the enormous gift that Christ purchased for us — the availability of choice and our freedom to choose.

He stops and looks around. SIR is poised with his finger on his ledger — he has all the time in the world. ANNA and FRANK have gone. HELEN, BEN and TINA have not heard a word he has said. His rally falters.

So that what I'm saying is — is that at this point there isn't necessarily an incompatability between your attitude, Sir, and my own —

SIR Good. 'It is 1.45 a.m. and — '

TOM And, Sir.

SIR looks at him.

(*Forced roguishness*) Keep watching — you're going to be surprised.

He leaves.

SIR 'It is 1.45 a.m. and Miriam and Charlie are at home, in bed. Charlie is sleeping. Miriam is staring at the ceiling. In the camp the reception is just over. Frank

Butler and the Minister of Defence and the Chief of Staff are standing in a corner, conversing privately. Father Tom is in the car park, searching his pockets for car keys. Anna is standing alone at the mess waiting for Frank. In the Butler living-room — '

He breaks off because his eye catches CHARLIE, *dressed as usual, tiptoeing across the stage.* CHARLIE *senses the silence, smiles at* SIR, *touches his forehead with his index finger.*

CHARLIE (*Confidentially*) Carry on — pay no attention to me — I'll just nip over here — look on from that corner.

He begins walking again.

SIR I'm sorry.

CHARLIE Fascinating to watch people — observe them, you know — just like in the courts — as long as you're not involved yourself — how the other half lives sort of thing.

SIR It is 1.45 a.m. You arrived at 11.30 and left with Miriam.

CHARLIE Honest to God, you won't hear a cheep out of —

SIR You're at home in bed. You're asleep and Miriam's awake.

CHARLIE I know the reason for that! If she's sleeping she can't think. (*Pause*) I mean to say — if she's thinking she can't sleep. (*Begins moving*) Just for this next piece —

SIR Good night, Charlie.

CHARLIE *stops.*

Good night.

CHARLIE *looks at him, sees he is adamant, and leaves.*

'In the Butler living-room the doors and windows are wide open because the night is sultry. Helen and Ben have a few drinks together.' I'll leave it to yourselves.

He retires to his stool. The lights change. The lights from the living-room spill out to the garden. BEN *and* HELEN *are slightly intoxicated and completely relaxed. This must not be played as a drunk scene, but lightly, full of laughter.* BEN *is striding about with a glass in his hand, a cigarette in his mouth. The diffident, uncertain* BEN *is suddenly voluble. The scene is played in almost constant movement — around the living-room, out in the garden, around the garden. Wherever* BEN *and* HELEN *go,* TINA *follows. But their accord, their intimacy, excludes her.*

BEN Follow behind me, keep me in sight, and I'll lead you there.

HELEN I'm on your heels.

BEN Right. Do you happen to remember a place by the name of Carrickfad?

HELEN Carrickfad! Do I remember Carrickfad!

BEN Good. So you pass Carrickfad. Turn right at the old coastguard station. Pass the old lime kiln. Pass the old rectory.

HELEN Ruins — ruins — ruins!

BEN Cross the wooden bridge and straight down that track until you come to the ringfort —

HELEN On your left when you're facing the sea.

BEN Turn left there, carry on for three-quarters of a mile until you come to the sand dunes —

HELEN In Culhame.

BEN Culhame is correct. But you have still to find my hermitage. Now, when you get to the foot of the sand hills, you stop, face north-north-west and look straight ahead; and if you've very good eyesight you'll see rising out of the bent the roof of a little blue caravan.

HELEN (*To* TINA) 'A secret place', he says!

BEN And there I can be consulted any morning between the hours of nine and eleven, except on those occasions when I'm off lecturing.

He goes out to the garden. HELEN *follows. Then* TINA.

HELEN Secret! I could make my way there now — in the dark!

TINA I was never there.

HELEN Didn't we spend every Sunday in the summer sliding down those same dunes!

TINA Had you great fun?

BEN And when I'm travelling abroad I can usually be contacted at the nearest Salvation Army hostel. You know, we old army types — a great freemasonry. (*Calls in the direction of camp*) My greetings, Chief of Staff, Adjutant General and Quartermaster General! God bless you, Number One Army Band!

HELEN They've left hours ago, clown!

BEN And warmest wishes to you, magazine, parade square and flagpole!

HELEN D'you remember the day the two of us climbed up onto the roof of the old coastguard station?

BEN A mad, mad pair!

TINA Was Miriam with you?

BEN Mad!

HELEN She went to the top of the walls but didn't go up onto the roof.

TINA And what happened?

HELEN (*To* BEN) Tell her what happened!

BEN What happened was that we were stuck up there for six hours.

HELEN Right!

BEN The pair of us clinging to two charred rafters.

HELEN Remember them groaning!

BEN Rigid with fright — couldn't move either forward or back in case they'd snap.

HELEN Mother calling up, 'Don't wriggle, Ben. Don't wriggle!'

BEN I was shaking with *cold*. And if I opened my eyes I could see Father directly below me. And cute enough, I remember thinking: if the rafter does snap, he'll break my fall.

HELEN Oh my God.

TINA How did you get down?

BEN It took a full detachment of engineers — scaffolding, generators, arc lights — the biggest peacetime operation ever mounted by Western Command. And an

	ambulance —
HELEN	Two ambulances!
BEN	And that old MO — Colonel — ?
HELEN	Hayes.
BEN	That's him. 'Where the hell are the blankets?'
HELEN	What a day — what a day!
TINA	You must have had a lot of fun.
HELEN	I don't know what I'm laughing at. I thought I was finished.
BEN	I pointed it out to Anna about a month ago — one day we were out at the caravan — and told her the whole escapade; but somehow there was none of the terror, none of the delight. (*Goes inside*) Now I have a feeling that if my commandant father knew I was here, he'd rush home and throw his arms around me and say, 'Welcome, son. Help yourself to a drink.'

HELEN *goes inside.* TINA *follows.*

HELEN	Part of him probably wants to.
BEN	Offer me a drink?
HELEN	You know very well.
BEN	'A large whiskey, Sir? Thank you very much, Sir. You're altogether too kind.'
HELEN	And if he did?

Pause as BEN *pours a drink.*

BEN	Too late — too late.
HELEN	But if he did?
BEN	We're long beyond that.
HELEN	What if he did?
BEN	What if he did? After all that's been said?
HELEN	Despite all that.
BEN	The day she died I called him a murderer.
HELEN	Six years have passed.
BEN	And he hit me — don't you remember? — he hit me!
HELEN	That's all over.
BEN	Years, years of hostility.
HELEN	That fades.

BEN Does it?
HELEN You know it does.
BEN You can preserve it.

> *He goes outside again. She follows. As before,* TINA *tags along.*

HELEN Why would you want to?
BEN In case you'd forget.
HELEN No!
BEN Out of a sense of loyalty.
HELEN To whom?
BEN You can embalm it consciously, deliberately —
HELEN That would be wrong.
BEN — in acts of terrible perfidy —
HELEN You wouldn't do that, Ben.
BEN — which you do in a state of confusion, out of some vague residual passion that no longer fires you; hitting out, smashing back, not at what's there but at what you think you remember; and which you regret instantly — oh, yes, yes, yes, never underestimate the regret. But then it's too late, too late — the thing's preserved in perpetuity — as Charlie would say.
HELEN You shouldn't drink.
BEN So as we used to say — put that in your pipe and smoke it.
HELEN (*To* TINA) Going off his head in that hermitage of his.
BEN Helen.
HELEN You *are* drunk.
BEN Sister Helen.
HELEN Sit down on that seat.
BEN Helen Sarah Fidelma.
HELEN H.S.F. — yes, I remember.
TINA What was that?
HELEN Horrible Smelly Feet.
TINA I never heard that before!
HELEN He used to drive me mad with that.
TINA I'm going to remember that — H.S.F!
BEN I want to tell you something.
HELEN You're getting silly.

BEN   I am not. And I want to tell you something.

HELEN   (*To* BEN) Give me a cigarette.

TINA   No, Helen, no!

HELEN   Just one.

BEN   Honourable Sincere Friend.

TINA   Don't, Helen, please.

BEN   We'll both have one.

TINA   You'll regret it, Helen.

BEN   I've something to say to you.

HELEN   Is it important?

BEN   Very important — vitally important — and you'll know it's important.

HELEN   How?

BEN   Because I'll probably start stammering in the middle of it!

They all laugh at this.

HELEN   Give me a light.

TINA   I'm disappointed in you, Helen.

HELEN   (*Mocking*) She's disappointed in me! Now I'm really upset. (*To* BEN) D'you remember — out in the turf shed — passing the cigarette from one to the other and it hot with sucking!

BEN   What I'm going to tell you is a big secret.

HELEN   I hate secrets.

BEN   No, not really a secret.

HELEN   Make up your mind.

BEN   More a confidence than a s-s-s-secret.

They all laugh.

HELEN   You faked that!

BEN   I did not!

HELEN   You did — to hook me!

TINA   Tell us your secret.

BEN   May I confide my confidence?

HELEN   You may not.

BEN   I'm going to tell you.

HELEN   I don't want to hear it.

BEN Helen —
HELEN Everybody tells me their confidences.
BEN Please —
HELEN I'm sick of their confidences.
BEN It's about —
HELEN (*Covering her ears*) No, no, no, no!
TINA (*Laughing*) Tell me, Ben! Tell me!
BEN It has to do with my embalming job.
HELEN Can't hear a word you're saying!
BEN (*Shouts*) And with my profound regrets.
HELEN We all have our regrets. Look after your own.
BEN I'll shock you, Helen.

> HELEN *takes her hands away from her ears. The atmos-
> phere suddenly changes: the laughing is finished.*

HELEN (*Imperious*) I want a cup of coffee! He needs a cup of
coffee! Go and make it for me, Tina!
BEN Mother's voice — exactly!
TINA I want to hear what Ben's —
HELEN (*Calmer*) Would you, darling, please?

> *She looks firmly at* TINA *until* TINA *finally gives way
> and goes into the living-room. She is about to go into
> the kitchen but hesitates to listen.*

On a night like this you can hear the sea breaking on
the Tor Mór.
BEN (*Quiet, urgent*) I've got to tell you, Helen.
HELEN You've 'got to' nothing.
BEN When you wanted to talk about your Gerry I listened
to you.
HELEN Years ago. For God's sake, you're a man now!
BEN I was the one carried your messages.
HELEN Stop bleating! Stop snivelling!
BEN Stood watching outside the gym hall when you and he
were inside. Warned you that night the two of you
took the jeep and went to the dance in Omagh —
HELEN And stood there at Mother's side — and held her hand
— held her hand as if you were her husband, while he

52

stood at the door with his cap in his hand, trembling, the fool, trembling because the Commandant's wife was quizzing him in her quiet and most reasonable voice about his 'educational background' and his father's 'profession' and his 'prospects in his chosen career' — Private Gerald Kelly, batman — my Gerry — *my* Gerry. And all the time you stood beside her in that wicker chair, facing him, stroking her hand. *You* did, Ben; yes, you. And d'you know what he did when he came outside? Gerald Kelly — the defiant, reckless, the daredevil Gerry Kelly? He cried, Ben. Yes; like a child. Gerry Kelly cried. Yes. He cried. Yes.

She goes to the other end of the garden. She cries quietly. BEN *goes to her.*

BEN I'm sorry, Helen.

HELEN (*Simply*) Sorry? What's sorry? 'Never underestimate the regret.' Is that what you said? I've lost him. She killed him. He's gone. Do I love Gerry Kelly still? I thought I'd squeezed every drop of him out of me. But now I know I haven't forgotten a second of him.

BEN Helen —

Pause. Then SIR *rises and moves forward.*

SIR Thank you. We've got quite a bit done. I'd say the back's broken. (*To audience*) We'll resume again in approximately — what? — fifteen minutes.

Quick black.

ACT TWO

Only MIRIAM *is onstage, sitting in the wicker chair, reading* The Donegal Enquirer, *eating a slice of cake, an empty coffee mug beside her.*

Great bursts of laughter come from the kitchen. And as the other characters come on they carry with them an air of good humour — a gaiety, or, as SIR *calls it, a 'giddiness' that permeates the beginning of this sequence, right up until the arrival of* SIR. *They are dressed as we saw them at the end of Act One, except* FRANK, *who is in desert uniform.* TINA, *laughing, opens the kitchen door.*

TINA There's a few cream cakes left. Do you want one?

MIRIAM Don't tempt me.

TINA Or a doughnut?

MIRIAM Please. I'm up to here. What are they laughing at?

TINA Father Tom's telling stories about when he was a curate in Yorkshire.

MIRIAM God, weren't we reared on them!

TINA Daddy says he makes them up as he goes along.

MIRIAM Listen to this — from the *Enquirer* — 'Commandant Butler's eldest daughter, Christina, is in London —'

TINA Me!

MIRIAM 'His youngest daughter, Helen, lives at home.'

TINA Sure they never get anything right, that crowd.

MIRIAM But wait till you hear this. 'And another daughter is married to Mr Charles Donnelly, who is popular in the legal and sporting life of Donegal. As a young man he was a well-known amateur high-jumper and is the father of three children!'

TINA (*Laughing*) I'm away back to London.

She returns to the kitchen.

MIRIAM High-jumper — sweet God. Amateur — my foot!

> *She continues reading.* BEN *enters left, singing, and meets* ANNA, *who enters from upstage — throughout this sequence none of the characters obeys the conventions of the set. They meet in the garden area.*

BEN We're not late, are we?

ANNA I don't think so.

BEN I suppose he'd be out clapping his hands for us. Come along, children, come along, come along.

> ANNA *sits on the garden seat.*

You're eager to get it over with, aren't you?

ANNA At the beginning I was. Now I don't care. Are you?

BEN I don't give a damn about anyone or anything. I feel . . . flushed, giddy . . . I feel euphoric. (ANNA *laughs*)

ANNA 'Euphoric'!

BEN I do. I haven't felt like this since — (*Stops*)

ANNA When?

BEN I can tell you exactly — six years ago, October 19th — the day of my mother's funeral. That's when. That afternoon. After we had come back from the cemetery. Shocking, isn't it?

ANNA Tell me about it.

BEN Nothing much to tell. We were all in there (*living-room*) — it was pouring with rain — there were some visitors — the girls were crying — everybody was whispering. And suddenly I had to rush out of the room because I was afraid I'd burst out singing or cheer or leap into the air. Honestly. Walked across the sand hills for maybe a couple of hours — I don't remember. Anyhow until that madness passed.

ANNA Was it madness?

> *Pause. He looks at her quickly. Then resumes as before.*

BEN And then I came back. Guilty as hell and soaked to the skin. (*Smiling*) And assumed the grief again — a greater grief, a guilty grief. All very strange.

ANNA Are you going to sing for us now?

BEN Sing, dance, anything you like.

> *He does a few extravagant leaps around the stage, singing a few lines of 'Singing in the Rain' at the same time. In the middle of his performance* MIRIAM *shouts out.*

MIRIAM Ben, will you — for the love of God!

ANNA (*When he finishes*) Very good. Very impressive.

> *He flops down beside her.*

BEN I really am giddy now!

ANNA I think you should stick to the fishing all the same.

BEN What are you going to do — when it's all over?

ANNA An aunt of mine has a café in New Jersey. She always wanted me over. So I'll stay with her for six months — until I've saved some money. Then I'll move on to San Francisco or Los Angeles; more likely San Francisco.

BEN Just like that?

ANNA Yes.

BEN Have you any relatives in California?

ANNA No.

BEN Do you know anybody there?

ANNA No one.

BEN God, I wish I could be as decisive as that.

ANNA What'll you do?

BEN When this is all over? Oh, I'll — I suppose I'll head off, too.

ANNA To America?

BEN Not America. America's too — too foreign for me. Scotland. England, maybe. Somewhere. Who knows?

ANNA But you'll keep coming back here, won't you?

> *Great laughter from the kitchen.*

BEN Are you laughing at me, too?

ANNA But that's what you'll do, isn't it?

BEN *leaps up.*

BEN   Let's go and see what's so funny.
ANNA   Oh, Ben, there's one thing I'd like you to do for me —
BEN   Yes?
ANNA   If you would.
BEN   What's that?
ANNA   You look startled.
BEN   Why should I look startled? What is it?
ANNA   I left a pair of old flat shoes in the caravan — I think
       they're in that press under the sink. And a blue and
       white scarf — it's hanging behind the door.
BEN   I'll get them for you.
ANNA   That's all.
BEN   Fine.

> *She goes up to him and kisses him lightly on the
> forehead.*

ANNA   Dismiss.
BEN   (*Uneasy laugh*) What's that for?
ANNA   Our attempt at a love affair.

> *Laughter from kitchen.*

BEN   What do you mean — attempt?
ANNA   That's what it was, wasn't it? (*She takes his arm and
       leads him into the living-room*) Come on — we're
       missing the fun.

> *As they enter, the others* — FRANK, TOM, TINA, HELEN
> — *emerge from the kitchen. Now that they are all
> together the euphoric atmosphere is heightened.*

FRANK I don't believe a word of it, Tom!
TOM   Would I tell a lie, Helen?
HELEN I keep telling you — I believe you.
FRANK He now suddenly remembers that Canon Bradshaw
        had a wooden leg!
MIRIAM God forgive you, Father Tom!

TOM May I be called before my Maker.
ANNA Who's Canon Bradshaw?

> FRANK *is standing beside* ANNA, *his arm casually around her shoulders.*

FRANK An eccentric parish priest he had when he was a curate in Hull.

TOM A terrific yoke made from Parana pine and treated with linseed oil. And he had two types of ferrule that he could screw into the bottom: one was brass that he used to polish every Friday night when he was doing the candlesticks —

HELEN He's remembering more details.

MIRIAM More lies.

BEN Let him tell the story.

FRANK (*To* ANNA) This was his first post.

TOM — and the other ferrule was wooden and covered with black astrakhan —

> *Great laughter.*

BEN Astrakhan?

TOM Just like a drumstick.

MIRIAM This is all new! Canon Bradshaw used to be a cripple in a wheelchair!

TOM God's my judge. And he'd use the wooden one when he'd be saying Mass upstairs in the oratory. And when he'd come to the Sanctus he'd suddenly kick out backways, just like a donkey, and bang the bell three times with the astrakhan head.

BEN Boom-boom-boom.

> *Laughter.*

FRANK Tom! Tom!

TINA When did he use the brass one?

HELEN You're encouraging him.

MIRIAM Try to stop him.

TOM He used the brass one —

MIRIAM This is definitely a lie.

TOM No. He used the brass one for walking, of course. And for beating carpets.

Again they all laugh.

I know — I know — no one ever believes me.

HELEN All that laughing — my sides are sore.

FRANK We're all sore. What has made all of us so frivolous?

MIRIAM Listen — listen — listen — have you all seen this (*paper*)?

BEN What is it?

FRANK Yes, study that. I look very distinguished in that.

TINA I think so too, Daddy.

FRANK (*To* ANNA) Have you seen it?

ANNA It's very good.

BEN Let me see.

MIRIAM Make up captions for the two of them as they shake hands. What's the President thinking? What's Father thinking?

TOM Hannibal's old eyes; and the way he's leaning slightly backways. You're thinking: the cute hawk smells the brandy off my breath!

HELEN Very good. Anna?

ANNA Show me.

FRANK You be careful now.

ANNA The President's saying to himself: my God, I've forgotten! Footman, Batman, Butler — what's the man's *name*?

FRANK If you want to know he called me Francis.

BEN I know what he's thinking: today's Monday — this must be the Italian equestrian team.

MIRIAM And what's Father thinking?

FRANK You'd never guess.

HELEN Tell us.

MIRIAM I know — I know: he keeps calling me Corporal — have I been demoted?

FRANK Wrong — wrong — all wrong.

HELEN All right — we give up — you tell us.

FRANK I will not.

MIRIAM Go. Go on.

SEVERAL }
TOGETHER } Come on, Father. Tell us. Tell us. We're dying to know.

FRANK No.

TOM He can't tell because it's obscene.

FRANK As a matter of fact —

HELEN Well?

FRANK (*To* ANNA) I was looking for you in the crowd.

> *This is greeted with clapping and with joking 'ohs' and 'ahs'.*

That's the truth.

TOM In that case, and with that set to your jaw your caption should read: 'If she's not here, I'll shoot her!' (*As he goes off*) Anybody for more coffee? My wonderful coffee?

SEVERAL }
TOGETHER } No! No! No! No! No! No!

TOM All right. All right.

> FRANK *takes advantage of the chorus to catch* ANNA *by the hand and lead her out to the garden. As he leads her out:*

FRANK Tom and his silly stories. He can spin them out for hours on end. (*He catches both her hands and holds her at arm's length*) Let me look at you. My God, how I missed you. Were they kind to you when I was away? Does the family overwhelm you? Did you miss me? Let me look at you. Let me look at my beautiful, beautiful mascot.

ANNA What do you see?

FRANK What's the serious face for?

ANNA Tell me what you see, Frank.

FRANK I see youth, beauty, directness, simplicity. My wife.

ANNA Anything else?

FRANK An ageing man trembling before her.

ANNA Why is he trembling?

FRANK With intensity. With uncertainty. Because he has never had joy like this. Because he is afraid that somehow he can't cope with so great a joy because he is an ageing man.

ANNA She is trembling too —

He puts his fingers across her lips.

FRANK Because he wants to smother her, wash her in words of love, but he can't because he has no fluency in love words and he's afraid she won't understand that —

Again she tries to speak and again he stops her.

No, no, no. And he's trembling because he's afraid she'll tire of a man so staid, so formal, so ponderous — tire of his earnestness — my God of this! — tire of this solemn, abject display that is the only method he knows. But you'd tell me if I ever began to disgust you, wouldn't you, Anna? Yes, you would. You'd have nothing to say — those eyes would tell me. (*Quick laugh*) I've a confession to make. Let's sit down.

They sit on the summer seat.

There are nine men in this country who know everything about you!

ANNA What men?

FRANK The men that I rescued in the desert. Each time I crawled back to base with a man on my back — each trip took about half an hour — I told him about you — everything about you — your hair, your neck, your shoulders, the way you laugh — everything. Luckily most of them were too ill to listen. Not that that made any difference — I'd have told them anyway. And one of them — fellow called Driscoll, lost both his legs — I had to carry him like a baby — he kept moaning and crying for his mother and I heard myself shouting to him, 'Shut up, Driscoll! I'm talking to you about my Anna! So shut up! Shut up!' And he did. And he listened. So you probably saved Driscoll's life — just as you have saved mine.

MIRIAM *comes out.*

MIRIAM D'you know what Charlie was saying? You should put
down spuds in this garden next year. Great for killing
weeds.

ANNA Where's Father Tom?

BEN, HELEN *and* TINA *come out to the garden.*

MIRIAM In the kitchen, I think.

HELEN You don't want more of his coffee, do you?

Laughter.

BEN Every time I hear Uncle Tom mention coffee I think of
that famous picnic years ago —

HELEN On Portnoo pier!

BEN That's it.

MIRIAM And the two flasks! Oh, sweet Saviour!

FRANK He'll hear you, Miriam.

TINA What was that? What happened?

FRANK It's a bit unkind to poor Tom.

BEN Poor Tom! I might have been killed.

MIRIAM (*To* ANNA) We all drove out to Portnoo this Sunday — oh,
thirteen — fourteen years ago —

BEN I was twelve at the time.

FRANK (*To* ANNA) The place with the lookout post on the hill
above it.

HELEN (*To* ANNA) Haven't you been there?

ANNA Yes, yes, I know it.

MIRIAM And Mammy sat with a rug round her knees and the rest
of us had a swim and then we spread the cloth out on the
pier for the picnic and Uncle Tom had his stuff and we
had ours. And it must have been the month of June
because I have a distinct memory that it was the first
strawberries we'd had that season and Mammy had a
carton of cream, fresh cream, and a carton of ice cream,
and you know that sensation when you taste the first
fresh strawberries of the season — just like the first new
spuds — only lighter and —

BEN   Tell the story, will you?

HELEN   We had just begun to eat —

MIRIAM   When suddenly Ben began behaving very strangely.

TINA   Oh, *that* story!

> SIR *enters; listens to the story and reacts to it as the others do. As the narrative unfolds,* BEN *acts the part he played.*

BEN   Hic-hup-hic-hic-hic.

MIRIAM   Staggering across the cloth and kicking over the cups and the strawberries and the ice cream; and of course Mammy began to panic —

FRANK   (*To* ANNA) We can laugh at it now.

HELEN   'Epilepsy! My baby boy's got epilepsy!'

TINA   The twelve-year-old baby!

FRANK   It was very frightening.

MIRIAM   And then he fell on his face and started vomiting and Mammy began to cry and Tina started to scream —

TINA   No wonder!

MIRIAM   All into the car — back home like the hammers of hell — and you know those roads along the Gweebarra —

FRANK   She knows them.

HELEN   (*To* BEN) You'd passed out at that stage and Uncle Tom was praying in your ear —

MIRIAM   Straight into sick-quarters — frantic phone calls — doctors and nurses summoned —

ANNA   What was it? What had happened?

MIRIAM   What had happened was that little Christina here —

TINA   I was six at the time!

MIRIAM   — had switched Uncle Tom's flask and our flask —

BEN   (*To* TINA) Monster!

MIRIAM   — and poor Mammy had given Ben a cup of neat whiskey!

ANNA   No!

HELEN   Almost killed him.

BEN   He was never the same since.

ANNA   Oh, poor Tom!

BEN   Oh, poor me!

MIRIAM   And of course he could never own up.

HELEN   Did he know?

MIRIAM	Did he know! Course he knew!
FRANK	The sequel's the best part. Tell her that.
HELEN	That bit's not true, Father.
FRANK	Is it not?
MIRIAM	Doesn't matter if it's true or not — it's part of the Butler lore.
ANNA	What's the sequel?
MIRIAM	Ben claims that —
BEN	I do not!
MIRIAM	All right — it is said that when he was lying in sick-quarters after he'd had his stomach pumped —
FRANK	Shhhh!
MIRIAM	— Uncle Tom came to see him.
BEN	That bit's true.
MIRIAM	— leaned over him, caught him by the throat, and said, 'Touch my flask again and I'll break your bloody neck!'

> *They all laugh at this. Then continue talking in undertones.* CHARLIE *enters and stops beside* SIR *who is laughing too.*

CHARLIE	What's all the laughing about?
SIR	Sorry?
CHARLIE	What are they laughing at?
SIR	They are happy.
CHARLIE	*They* are?
SIR	Yes.
CHARLIE	They know what's going to happen, don't they?
SIR	They know.
CHARLIE	So what are they happy about?
SIR	There's always a gaiety at this stage.
CHARLIE	At what stage?

> SIR *is walking towards the family. He is smiling. He does not look at* CHARLIE.

SIR	Sorry?
CHARLIE	What episode is that?
SIR	Look at them — they're so happy.

CHARLIE When is this supposed to have taken place?

SIR Yes, I'm afraid they've taken a few liberties.

CHARLIE Is this in your book?

SIR Some of it is, Charlie. And I'm afraid some of it is the wishful thinking of lonely people in lonely apartments. But they're always being true to themselves. And even if they've juggled the time a bit, they're doing no harm. We mustn't be impatient with them.

CHARLIE Cracked, that family. Bloody cracked. Always was. And it's the same with my woman every time she gets back among them — she's as bad as they are. Look at her for God's sake! I don't see much of that side of her when she's at home, I can tell you.

He leaves quickly. SIR *now joins the others.*

TINA Here's Sir!

SIR Carry on — carry on — don't let me interrupt.

FRANK Just recalling a family outing.

SIR Yes.

MIRIAM A picnic years ago.

SIR The famous day at Portnoo — I know — I know.

The gaiety ebbs quickly away.

HELEN I don't think we ever went back there, did we?

BEN I didn't.

HELEN Not as a family group.

MIRIAM Not for a picnic.

HELEN Certainly not for a picnic.

TINA I was there one day last Easter. By myself.

FRANK And Anna and I have gone a few times, haven't we?

ANNA Where to?

FRANK Portnoo.

ANNA Yes — once or twice.

FRANK Just for the run. But no picnic, I'm afraid.

SIR It's a pretty place, Portnoo.

FRANK Lovely on a good day.

SIR Beautiful. And across the bay there's an attractive little island.

FRANK Inniskeel — is that what it's called?

SIR That's it.

FRANK Yes.

SIR And when the tide's out, you can walk out to it — out to the island.

FRANK So I believe — I've never done that.

SIR Actually you don't walk out from Portnoo. You go from Narin just over the road.

FRANK I see. No, I've never done that.

SIR Yes. A pretty place, Portnoo. Very pretty place.

Pause.

ANNA Shouldn't we get on with it?

SIR Take your time — I'm in no hurry.

FRANK Perhaps we should.

SIR There's no rush.

MIRIAM Yes, let's start.

FRANK I think we should.

SIR If you would like to make a fresh pot of tea or — ?

ANNA Let's start! Let's start!

SIR Whatever you say . . .

FRANK Yes, the sooner the better.

SIR Very well. (*Opens his ledger*) Where would you like to resume? (*Waits — no answers*) Anyone got any preference?

TOM *bursts in from the kitchen.*

TOM I've remembered another use he had for that brass ferrule. You know how people in chapel like to sit spread out in those long pews? Well, he used to go hopping up along the aisle and whatever unfortunate was at the end of the seat he'd prod him — (*Sees SIR*) Oh! You're back!

SIR Only a few minutes — that's all.

TOM (*Looking around*) Are we ready to — to go?

SIR If you are.

TOM Me. Oh, I'm — certainly, certainly. Any time you're ready, I'm — I'm — (*He fades out*)

SIR If no one else has any suggestions, may I propose that we do the reasonable thing — in other words carry on almost immediately after we left off; that is to say, just before the return of Frank and Anna and Tom from the reception. Does that suit everybody?

No answer.

And Tom!

TOM Sir?

SIR (*Smiling*) I'll keep watching.

TOM (*Uneasily*) Oh yes, yes, do — do that.

TOM *exits quickly — in his confusion going off left instead of right.*

SIR Not that way, Tom. Over this — (TOM *has gone*) I don't think we need those things, do we?

He picks up empty coffee mugs, the Enquirer; *adjusts the chairs.*

MIRIAM I'm not needed, am I?

SIR Not for the time being, thank you. Nor Helen, nor Tina. (*Looking round the set*) That's more like it, isn't it?

SIR *returns to his stool.* HELEN *and* TINA *and* MIRIAM *move off. Then* ANNA. *Finally* FRANK. FRANK *is thinking himself back to the scene that* SIR *has called for. As he passes* BEN:

BEN Talking about that silly picnic —

FRANK (*To himself*) Let's see. We left the mess. I drove. Anna was beside me. Tom was in the back —

BEN No, no, the Portnoo picnic — coming home in the car — you were driving and I was lying across Mother's lap — I suppose I was drunk, for God's sake —

FRANK (*Only now aware of him*) What's that?

BEN And you k-k-k- — and you kept —

SIR 'It is now 3.45 a.m. — '

BEN My head was on your knees — and you had one hand on the driving wheel — and your other hand kept s-s-s-s- — your other hand kept —

SIR Frank.

FRANK Sir?

SIR You're off at this point.

FRANK Yes, I know that. (*Irritably to* BEN) What is it? What is it?

BEN With your other hand, your free hand, all the way home you kept stroking my face, my face, my cheeks, my forehead —

SIR Gentlemen, I'm sorry. I must insist.

FRANK (*To* BEN) Not now, later, please —

BEN But what I want to tell you, Father, and what I want you to know is that I —

FRANK (*Leaving*) Some other time.

SIR 'It is now 3.45 a.m. Tina is sleeping in bed. Helen is getting her case ready. Frank, Anna and Tom are driving home from the reception — Frank and Anna in front, Tom in the back — '

He is interrupted by TOM, *who has discovered that he exited the wrong way. He is now crossing in front of* SIR.

TOM Sorry — sorry — beg your pardon.

SIR Take your time. No rush.

TOM Looking for matches.

SIR And did you get some?

TOM *taps his jacket pocket.*

Fine — fine. No hurry. We've all the time in the world. (*Calls*) Ready now, Frank?

FRANK (*Off*) Yes.

SIR (*Calls*) And Anna?

ANNA (*Off*) Ready.

SIR Good. Where was I? Ah — ' — Tom in the back. Ben is alone in the living-room. He is moving around.' And that seems to be all the directions I've got. A bit abrupt, isn't it? Could you carry on from there? Thank you.

He sits on his stool. The lights change. BEN *is alone in the living-room.*

BEN   There was a fellow in my class at UCD; Sproule — Harry Sproule; from Tipperary. Horsey people. Had a brother doing Arts and another doing Law at the same time. And each had a flat of his own. And the three of them never met during term — not even once. Didn't even travel together. Strange, wasn't it? Harry Sproule. (*He fingers the ornament*)

HELEN   (*Off*) What's that?

BEN   Called his father and mother by their Christian names. Spoke of them warmly — as if they were friends of the family. (*Pause*) Did you ever think what it must have been like for Anna coming into our family?

He circles around the wicker chair, looking at it.

HELEN   (*Off*) I can't hear you.

BEN   (*Not as loud*) With our bloody boring reminiscences and our bloody awareness and our bloody quivering sensibilities. There must be another way of ordering close relationships, mustn't there? (*Shouts*) Mustn't there?

HELEN *enters. A cigarette in her mouth. Very brisk. She lifts a book and then goes to the radiator, where her tights are spread.*

HELEN   Mustn't there what?

BEN   I'm saying we're a very closely knit family.

HELEN   I don't know. Are we? I suppose so. Does it matter? Tights drying on a radiator and no heating on!

BEN   Maybe I should go now, Helen.

HELEN   Go where?

BEN   Leave. Before they get back.

HELEN   Whatever suits you.

BEN I'd just like to see him for one minute, give him my congratulations and then clear off.

HELEN (*Firmly*) Listen to me. You'll stay where you are. When he comes you'll shake his hand, say your piece, and then leave. Right? Can't wear these tomorrow.

BEN I think I'll take a drink. No, maybe I shouldn't. You'll be here, won't you?

HELEN What do you want me to do, Ben? Stand at your side and hold your hand and stroke it?

She rushes upstairs.

BEN Helen, I've already apologized —

But she is gone. He is wretched.

God! (*Rehearsing*) Congratulations, Sir, I'm really proud of — (*Pause*) Very well done, Frank. Great work. Splendid — (*Pause*) When I heard it on the radio, Father, I was so th-th-th-th-thrill — Oh Christ!

The voice of TOM *off. Approaching, singing very slowly and very drunkenly.*

TOM We're here because we're here because we're here because we're here.

BEN *rushes to the drinks. Uncorks a bottle, puts it to his head, corks it again. Then sits on the armchair right of fireplace.* TOM *arrives at the front door. He knocks loudly on it three times.* BEN *leaps up instinctively, nervously — then sits again.*

Right door — wrong house.

He stands back and examines the façade.

Right house — wrong door.

He begins singing again. Comes into the garden doing

an absurd advancing/retreating dance as he crosses the stage. Finally, very shortly after ANNA's *entrance, he falls into a deck chair and falls asleep. While* TOM *is dancing,* ANNA *enters. She goes straight into the living-room. At first she does not see* BEN.

BEN   You're very late.

ANNA   What are you doing here?

BEN   Just to congratulate —

ANNA   Get out! Get out!

BEN   What's wrong?

ANNA   My head's splitting — that's what's wrong! I'm at my wits' end — that's what's wrong!

> FRANK *enters the hallway. He is elated, assured, exuding confidence.*

FRANK   Helen! Helen!

ANNA   Get out, Ben, for God's sake!

> *Before* BEN *can make up his mind,* FRANK *enters.*

FRANK   I know she won't have gone to bed. She may have —

> *He stops suddenly when he sees* BEN. *They stand looking at one another. Pause.*

BEN   I was passing and I just dropped in . . . .

FRANK   Yes?

> *Pause.*

BEN   I heard all about it on the radio and read all the stuff in the papers — and for your sake I was really very — it was just great. (*Holds out his hand*) Congratulations.

FRANK   (*Very formally*) Thank you.

> *Then suddenly* FRANK *opens his arms and embraces* BEN *warmly.*

Ben! Thank you, son. Thank you.

HELEN *enters from kitchen.*

Do you see who's here?

HELEN   Naturally.

FRANK   Naturally.

HELEN   Well — how did it go? (*To* ANNA) Had you a great night? (*To* FRANK) You have news! I know by your face you have news!

FRANK   I had a wonderful night.

HELEN   Great.

He catches HELEN *in his arms and swings her round.*

FRANK   And I have wonderful news!

HELEN   (*To* ANNA) Tell me! (*To* FRANK) Tell me — tell me — tell me —

FRANK   Have a guess.

HELEN   Guess! How can I guess!

FRANK   But first we'll have a celebration drink. (*Looking at* BEN) A double celebration. (*Looking at* ANNA) A treble celebration.

ANNA   Where's Father Tom?

FRANK   Who cares?

HELEN   (*To* ANNA) He's being transferred, isn't he?

FRANK   Yes, he's being transferred.

BEN   Wonderful.

FRANK   Where would you like him to be transferred to?

HELEN   Where? Where?

FRANK   Guess.

HELEN   Ah, Father —

FRANK   Take your choice.

HELEN   Tell us! Athlone?

FRANK   Anywhere you like.

HELEN   Ben, where? (*To* FRANK) I know! Cork!

FRANK   Cork's for talkers.

BEN   You're going to Galway.

FRANK   Galway's for ageing men.

HELEN   Limerick!

FRANK   Good God! Never Limerick!

HELEN   Where else? — where else? — it's not! It couldn't be!

FRANK   Couldn't be what?

HELEN   Dublin?

FRANK   Dublin it is.

HELEN   Oh, Father!

She kisses him.

FRANK   (*To* ANNA) And tell them the rest.

ANNA   Better look out for Father Tom.

She goes out to the garden.

FRANK   You are in the presence of Lieutenant-Colonel Frank Butler —

HELEN   Lieutenant — ?

FRANK   Administrative Officer, GHQ, Parkgate Street, Dublin City.

HELEN   You're taking a hand at us, Father!

FRANK   Nothing's official yet. But when the Chief tells the Taoiseach in your presence how highly he considers you and then in the next breath talks about certain vacancies, you know it's in the bag.

HELEN   I'm going to waken Tina — phone Miriam —

FRANK   Later — later — later. Let's savour it ourselves first.

BEN   (*Looking around*) So you'll be leaving here.

FRANK   At last, at long last, and without one regret. To Dublin.

HELEN   To the Hero and to Anna.

BEN   To you, Father.

FRANK   Hold on — where's Anna?

HELEN   In the garden.

He goes to the door and looks out to the garden. ANNA *is crouched beside* TOM, *trying to waken him.*

FRANK   Let him sit there for God's sake. Come inside and celebrate with the family.

TOM   (*Suddenly awake, sings*) We're here because we're here because we're here because we're here —

HELEN So that's the condition.

ANNA (*To* TOM) Come inside and lie down for a while.

FRANK You're a bloody useless slob, Tom. Pull yourself together, man.

HELEN How did Anna enjoy it?

> FRANK *turns back into the living-room.* ANNA *gets* TOM *to his feet and they make their way slowly into the room,* TOM *singing intermittently.*

FRANK Anna? Anna was — what's the word? — cynosure of all eyes. Radiant, that's what Anna was, sitting there beside me, basking in the glory. And the compliments — my God! The Taoiseach called her — incidentally that was by far the best speech of the night. And astonishingly well informed — named every one of the soldiers I had saved and a few personal comments about several of them. And when he was talking about me — well, he was so effusive and so generous that I was almost embarrassed. Talked about 'quiet heroes from quiet places' and 'men whose full development blossomed only in full manhood'. Really eulogistic stuff. Very satisfying.

HELEN And Anna?

BEN Sit over here, Father.

FRANK That's the state he was in after the first course.

HELEN What did he say about Anna?

FRANK Oh, Anna? What's this he called you? — a real tongue-twister — 'the Commandant's comely, composed and curvaceous consort' — at which the men just *howled* Didn't they?

ANNA Yes.

FRANK Would you like to try that one, Ben?

BEN (*Quickly*) You're okay, Father. You're fine. That's it.

ANNA (*To* BEN) Could I get him something?

FRANK Let him sleep it off. He's beyond sobering.

TOM (*Suddenly awake*) Where's Helen? Want to 'pologize to Helen —

HELEN Hello, Father.

TOM (*Rising*) — 'pologize to Helen — privately — in here,

Helen, in here. (*Staggers into the kitchen*)

FRANK Ignore him.

HELEN Poor old Tom.

FRANK But the highlight of the evening, Helen — I was presented with an illuminated address by the people of Ballybeg!

TOM (*Off*) Helen!

FRANK The people of Ballybeg — my God! A parchment this length, all the colours of the rainbow, and a photo of me stuck crookedly on the top; and read out before everybody by that pompous TD — McLaughlin, McLucas, what's his name.

HELEN That was nice of them.

FRANK D'you think so? Yes, I suppose the intention was good. But being publicly addressed by the people of Ballybeg — 'you are our most illustrious citizen' sort of stuff — my God they don't know me and we don't know them! But you'll enjoy this — you really will. Must have left it out in the car. Hold on a second.

TOM (*Off*) Helen!

FRANK I know him in this mood. Ignore him.

FRANK *leaves.*

HELEN Have you ever seen him so elated! I'm delighted for him. (*She kisses* ANNA) For both of you. Was it exhausting? Are you falling apart?

TOM (*Off*) Helen!

HELEN Oh my God. (*Calls*) Coming! Coming!

She goes into the kitchen. Pause.

ANNA I can take no more of it.

BEN If you just —

ANNA I'm going to clear out in the morning.

BEN Leave him?

ANNA Didn't you hear him? 'I — I — I — I — I.' And how they howled — oh, how they howled — after sniggering behind their hands all night.

BEN At him?

ANNA Him — me — what matter? I can stand no more. I've got to go.

BEN Just walk out?

ANNA I've got to.

BEN Oh, Anna, you can't do that —

ANNA Why not?

BEN That — that would kill him — he'd never understand.

ANNA All right — I'll make him understand. You want him to understand?

BEN What I'm saying is that you just can't walk out without —

ANNA Fine. I'll tell him about us first.

BEN Anna —

ANNA You want him to understand?

BEN Will you please —

ANNA Do you think for one second he's not going to hear?

BEN For Christ's sake —

ANNA That the good people of Ballybeg or his own staff aren't going to let him know somehow?

BEN You won't!

ANNA Make up your mind! Is he not going to understand because he's not told? Or is he going to understand because he'll be told by them or by me — or by you, Ben?

BEN Nobody need say anything. I'll clear out in —

ANNA Yes, you'll clear out — typical Ben! What about me?

BEN I'm warning you, Anna.

ANNA Don't wag your finger at me!

BEN If you tell him —

ANNA Tell him — don't tell him — either way I'm leaving.

BEN I'm saying n-n-n-nothing. I promise you that. Nothing. Nothing. Nothing.

ANNA In that case I'll tell him. He deserves that much from me.

BEN You're a heartless bitch!

Enter HELEN *and* TOM, *arm in arm.*

HELEN Poor Father Tom. D'you know what that was all about? He officiated at all the Butler weddings and all

76

the Butler baptisms but he didn't officiate at Helen's wedding, even though Helen asked him, because Louise disapproved and he hadn't the courage to stand up to Louise and it has been on his conscience ever since and that's why he's drunk tonight — otherwise he'd be cold sober. So.

TOM Am I forgiven, Helen?

HELEN Nothing to forgive, Father.

TOM You know something, Helen?

HELEN What's that, Father?

TOM I'm no damn good, Helen. No damn good at all. I'm — I'm a washout, Helen.

HELEN Indeed you're not.

TOM You can't fool me, Helen, I know. I *know*.

HELEN You're fine, Father.

TOM And I'm forgiven?

HELEN Completely.

He slumps into a seat.

TOM Thanks be to God.

Almost immediately he is asleep.

HELEN There you are — instant absolution!

FRANK *enters reading in mock heroic style from the parchment. He begins at the front door.*

FRANK 'We, the people of Ballybeg, learn with great pride and great delight of the heroic deeds of Commandant Frank Butler' — Lieutenant-Colonel Butler, if you don't mind, Ballybeg — 'who is an honoured and distinguished member of our parish and whose family the people of Ballybeg have always held in the highest esteem.'

HELEN Read it properly, Father. Don't make a mock of it.

FRANK 'We have always known the Hero of Hari' — Who's that? I beg your pardon — 'to have been an officer of exemplary habit and behaviour, a citizen of outstanding probity — '

ANNA Frank.

FRANK ' — and a father and a family man' — I like this — 'of noblest Christian integrity and rectitude.'

ANNA Frank.

FRANK Get down on your knees. 'We are confirmed in our estimate, therefore, when the fame of his heroic actions spread out across the face of — '

ANNA I've something to say to you, Frank.

He stops and looks at her. TINA *comes sleepily downstairs in her dressing-gown and is about to enter when she hear's* ANNA's *voice. She stands outside the living-room door.*

I am not going to Dublin with you.

FRANK Nobody's going anywhere, my darling, until official confirmation comes.

ANNA Then — any time — I'm not going to Dublin — I'm not going anywhere with you.

Pause.

FRANK What is the matter, my love?

ANNA Are you deaf? Are you stupid? Don't you understand simple words? (*As he puts out his hand to her*) Don't — don't — don't touch me! I'm leaving you, Frank — can't you understand that? Leaving you — leaving you — is that simple enough?

Very long pause during which FRANK, *puzzled, studies her face for clues.*

HELEN I think she's —

FRANK What is wrong, Anna?

HELEN (*To* ANNA) You've had a very tiring —

FRANK (*Firmly*) Please, Helen. (*Quietly to* ANNA) Why are you leaving me, Anna? Is it something that I have said?

ANNA *turns away from him because she is crying. She*

shakes her head.

Is it something that I have done?

ANNA *shakes her head.*

HELEN Anna —
FRANK (*Very sharply*) Helen, please. (*Again quietly to* ANNA) Is
it something that I have not done?

ANNA *shakes her head.*

Then why are you leaving me, Anna?
ANNA You were so long away —
FRANK Five months.
ANNA And we'd been together such a short time —
FRANK Ten days.
ANNA (*Quickly*) And I tried to keep you, to maintain you in
my mind — I tried, Frank, I tried. But you kept
slipping away from me. I searched Tina for you, and
Miriam, but you weren't in them. And then I could
remember nothing — only your uniform, the colour of
your hair, your footstep in the hall — that's all I could
remember — a handsome, courteous, considerate
man who had once been kind to me and who wrote me
all those simple, passionate letters — too simple, too
passionate. And then Ben came. And I found you in
him, Frank.
FRANK Found me?
ANNA I was lost.

FRANK *looks at her, then at* BEN, *then back to her.*

FRANK Are you telling me that you and he — ?
ANNA We had an affair! We were lovers, Ben and I! And
everybody in the camp knows! Everybody in Ballybeg
knows! Everybody except the Butlers! That's what
I'm telling you! We had an affair!

TINA *gives a short cry — unheard in the living-room —*

79

and rushes upstairs.

HELEN Oh Ben! — you? — Oh God!

She turns away from him. FRANK *goes to* TOM *and puts his hand on the chaplain's shoulder.*

FRANK (*Softly*) Chaplain — Chaplain.
TOM Mmmm?
FRANK Help, Chaplain.
TOM (*Wakening*) Wha' — wha' — what's that?
FRANK Advice, counsel, help, Chaplain.
TOM What's the trouble, Frank?
FRANK I need help, Tom.
TOM Terrific, Frank — just terrific — terrific.
FRANK What does a man do, Tom?
TOM Yes, sir — yes, sir — just terrific.
FRANK What should a man do?

TOM is asleep again. FRANK *looks at him. Then very slowly he walks around the room as if he were trying to remember something. Finally, conversationally:*

You know, when I think about it — my God, how she must have suffered. Not that I was insensitive to it — far from it; I used to try to imagine what it was like. I would close my eyes and attempt to invest my body with pain, willing it into my joints, deliberately desiring the experience. But it's not the same thing — not the same thing at all — how could it be? Because it cannot be assumed like that — it has got to be organic, generated from within. And the statistics are fascinating too — well, no, not fascinating — how could they be fascinating; but interesting, interesting. It starts around forty; it's estimated that five to six per cent of the population is affected; and women are three times more susceptible than men. But there you are — she was outside the general pattern. What age was she? Helen was what? — three? — four? — so she can't have been more than twenty-eight or twenty-nine. And she had a very brief introductory period, as they call it. Within six months the hands and feet were swollen and within twelve months the spine was affected. So that within no time at all the fibrous tissues had replaced the normal tissues and when that happens you have at least a partial disorganization of the joints and sometimes complete ankylosis — yes, you'd think I was an authority —

HELEN Father —

FRANK — and of course we attempted everything that was available — physiotherapy, teeth, tonsils, surgery, gold injections, aspirin courses, codeine courses. We even went to a quack in Kerry who promised us that before we'd be halfway home every swelling would have disappeared. And the cortisone era — my God, the miracle era — the cure for everything. And she responded so wonderfully to it at first — absolutely no pain. She was even able to throw away the stick for a couple of weeks. But it was an illusion — an illusion. Back came the pain, worse than ever. Much, much worse. My God, how she suffered. My God, how she suffered.

He stops and looks at each person in the room. Then he looks out at SIR, *whom he now addresses loudly, very deliberately, and with conscious formality. He is very calm and very controlled.*

Sir.

SIR *speaks quietly and does not raise his eyes from the ledger.*

SIR Frank.

FRANK I wish to protest, Sir. I wish to lodge a formal protest.

SIR Yes, Frank.

FRANK I am quite calm. And I am not bleating. I am not snivelling.

SIR No, Frank.

FRANK But there are certain things that as a soldier — as a man

81

— I wish to state.

SIR Yes, Frank.

FRANK Yes, you did say we could speak our thoughts. That was established at the outset, wasn't it? Well, I wish to protest against my treatment. I wish to say that I consider I have been treated unfairly.

SIR (*Looking up*) Frank, I —

FRANK No, I'm not addressing you, Sir; I'm not addressing them; I suppose I'm not addressing anybody. And I am fully aware that protesting at this stage is pointless — pointless.

SIR You can —

FRANK No, no, no, of course it is. Absolutely pointless. The ledger's the ledger, isn't it? Nothing can be changed now — not a thing. But an injustice *has* been done to me, Sir, and a protest must be made. I don't claim that I have been blameless. Maybe my faults have been greater than most. But it does seem — well, spiteful that when a point is reached in my life, and late in my life, when certain modest ambitions are about to be realized, when certain happinesses that I never experienced are suddenly about to be attainable, it does seem spiteful that these fulfilments should be snatched away from me — and in a particularly wounding manner. Yes, I think that is unfair. Yes, that is unjust. And that is why I make this formal protest, Sir. Against an injustice done to me. Because I have been treated unfairly, Sir — that is all.

He stops and looks around at the others — all isolated, all cocooned in their private thoughts. He opens his mouth as if he is about to address them, but they are so remote from him that he decides against it. He turns slowly and begins to walk upstage.

SIR Frank!

FRANK *ignores the call and goes through the door right off the fireplace, closing it behind him — this is the only time this door is used. Pause. Suddenly* TOM, *now sober, jumps to his feet. He is very agitated, and when he looks at the others, so contained, so remote, his panic increases. He goes to* BEN.

TOM You're not going to let him go, are you? You're going to stop him, aren't you? For God's sake, Ben, you've got to stop him!

> BEN *remains encased and intact in his privacy.* TOM *looks to* HELEN *and goes to her.*

You know what's going to happen! You know what he's going to do! Stop him. Helen! Stop him! Stop him!

> *She looks at him as if he were a stranger.*

Don't you hear what I'm saying — he has got to be stopped!

> HELEN *looks away from him.* TOM *now addresses them all.*

How can you all sit there! You know what he's going to do!

> *No one responds.* TOM *now looks to* SIR — *and rushes to him. He is about to cry with panic and despair.*

You're going to stop him, aren't you, Sir? Yes, you're the one who can save him. You're not going to let him do that to himself — no, no, you're not.

SIR The ledger can't be —

TOM What can the ledger not be? — to hell with the ledger — that's what I say — to hell with that corrupt ledger.

SIR Tom, sit down —

TOM Great — great — 'Tom, sit down' — you know what Frank's going to do and all you can say is 'Tom, sit down'.

SIR Sit down and keep quiet.

TOM I will not sit down and I will not keep quiet! My friend, Frank, has gone into that back room and not one of you is going to —

SIR Shut up! Now!

TOM I will —

SIR You had your opportunities and you squandered them.

TOM I never had —

SIR Many opportunities, many times. You should have spoken then. We'll have none of your spurious concern now that it's all over. So sit down and shut up!

TOM (*Suddenly deflated*) If I had — sometimes, I — I always tried to — Oh, my Jesus —

For a few seconds his mouth keeps opening and shutting, but no words come. He looks at the others. Pause. Then he shuffles over to ANNA, *sits beside her, puts his arm round her, and rests his face on her shoulders. His body shakes as he cries quietly. Pause. Then suddenly* TINA *comes stumbling down the stairs in a panic and rushes into the living-room. She is in a frenzy and looks around wildly. Then:*

TINA (*Shouts*) Daddy-Daddy-Daddy-Daddy!

SIR *leaps to his feet.*

SIR (*Tense whisper*) Not yet! Tina! Not yet!

She freezes. Pause. Then a single revolver shot off. TINA's *hands go up to her face. She screams. Silence. Pause.* SIR *sits again. Then very slowly, the others relax and emerge from their cocoons. Cigarettes are lit. A sense of relief. Serenity. The remaining sequence must not be played in a sad, nostalgic mood.* MIRIAM *enters in coat and headscarf.* TOM, *now fully sober, sits with his arms around* ANNA. *From his stool* SIR *watches this slow awakening. Then he rises, stretching his arms, smiling.*

SIR Well — well — well — well — well — well — well.

He goes into the living-room.

That wasn't too bad, was it?

No one answers — they are still not quite out of their reveries. He goes to TINA, *catches her chin and wags it.*

And how are you? All right?

She smiles and nods.

(*To all*) That wasn't too bad after all now, was it? No, of course it wasn't. (*To* HELEN) And you with your worries that things were being 'distorted' — (*To* ANNA) — and you afraid that you'd 'messed it all up' — (*To both*) I told you, didn't I? Incidentally, Anna, we made a mistake, you and I — well me, really.

ANNA What was that?

SIR I never introduced you! You're the only person who wasn't introduced. (*Opening ledger*) So let's rectify that — right?

ANNA No, please, Sir —

SIR But I *want* to —

ANNA Please. It doesn't matter now, not in the least. It's of no importance now.

SIR I'm sorry. My mistake.

ANNA It doesn't matter.

SIR As you wish. (*He leafs through the ledger*) I'm sure you're all tired, so what I think we'll do is go straight to the postscript and wind it up with that. 'Not yet, Tina! Not yet! — Single revolver shot — etc., etc. — ' We've been through all that —

TOM There was never any doubt in my mind that it was an unfortunate accident. Never. And I said that at the inquest. I mean we were such terrific friends all our lives — no one was going to tell me that Frank Butler took — that it wasn't an accident. And I saw to it that my friend was buried with the full rites of the Church.

I saw to that. It was the least I could do for my friend, Frank Butler — my terrific friend, Frank.

SIR has been waiting patiently for this to end.

SIR Yes. A brief enough postscript as it happens. 'Funeral on Friday afternoon. The following morning Charlie Donnelly arrived with a van and removed all the furnishings —' By the way, where is Charlie? Charlie!

He goes off left to look for him.

MIRIAM I was worried about the children — you know — what I'd tell them.

TOM Naturally. And how are the kids?

MIRIAM I'd given them cornflakes and a fry for their breakfast — they're a great crowd for fries — and they were sitting round the table eating like nobody's business and I said quietly, 'Your Granda's dead,' I said. 'Your Granda's gone to heaven to join your Grandma,' I said. And when they began to cry I said, 'Don't cry for your Granda,' I said. 'Your Granda was a good man and a brave man. Ask anybody,' I said, 'and they'll tell you how good and brave your Granda was.' Wasn't I right, Father?

TOM God have mercy on his good soul.

MIRIAM And they listened to me. You should have seen them. They did — they listened — and they stopped crying. But he was a good man, you know — a good man and a brave man. No — a great man and a brave man.

She moves slowly off right.

SIR (*Off left*) Charlie! Charlie!

TOM You're going back to London, aren't you?

HELEN Tomorrow afternoon.

TOM Tina's going with you?

HELEN Yes.

TOM You'll look after her well, Helen, won't you? It's a big city and she's never been away from home and —

TINA Don't worry about me. I'll be all right. I can look after myself.

TOM You'll be in digs with Helen — that's good. And she'll get you fixed up in a job.

TINA I'm not a child, Father. I'm almost nineteen.

TOM All the same, my love —

TINA (*Bitterly*) Why the sudden concern about me. Why all the platitudes? You're the one in trouble, Father — not me.

> *She goes off quickly.*

HELEN She didn't mean that, Father. She's upset. Tina!

> *She follows* TINA *off.* SIR *enters.*

BEN (*Urgently*) Remember just before that last sequence?

SIR (*Consulting ledger*) Mm?

BEN I was going to say something to him and you interrupted.

SIR (*Not listening*) Yes — yes —

> TOM *looks around, then drifts aimlessly off.*

BEN Maybe I had some intimation of a moment being missed forever — because there was the sudden necessity to blurt out, to plunge some oversimplification into him before it was too late. And what I was going to say to him was that ever since I was a child I always loved him and always hated her — he was always my hero. And even though it wouldn't have been the truth, it wouldn't have been a lie either: no, no; no lie.

SIR I see.

BEN But I suppose it was just as well it wasn't said like that because he could never receive that kind of directness, and I suppose I could never have said it. But I just hope — I just hope he was able to sense an expression of some k-k-k-k- — of some kind of love for him — even if it was only in my perfidy —

He goes off slowly.

SIR Yes. (*Back to ledger*) ' — removed all the furnishings.'
Yes. 'That afternoon Helen and Tina flew to London,
where they now live in different flats and seldom
meet. Tina works as a waitress in an all-night café and
Helen has had to give up her office job because of an
acute nervous breakdown. Ben went to Scotland. He
came back after seven months. He has been jailed
twice for drunk and disorderly behaviour. Father Tom
has retired and is living in a nursing-home in County
Wicklow. He has difficulty walking and spends most
of his time in bed.'

CHARLIE's *brisk entrance interrupts the reading.*

CHARLIE Sorry — sorry — sorry — you were looking for me?
SIR It doesn't matter, Charlie. We're just finishing up.
CHARLIE If I'm here, I'm not wanted. (*Pause*) I mean to say — if
I'm wanted I'm not here. (*Laughs in surprise*) Dammit,
they're both right! First time that ever happened! Isn't
that a good one! Where's the missus?
SIR She left a few minutes ago.
CHARLIE Oh-ho! Better catch up with her or there'll be hair
flying. See you. Good luck — good luck. (*Pause at exit*)
When do I clear out this stuff?
SIR Saturday.
CHARLIE Morning or afternoon?
SIR Morning.
CHARLIE Bang goes the sleep-in. Oh, well, good to get it all out
of the road. Luck.

He leaves.

SIR Goodbye, Charlie. Now — ' — spends most of his
time in bed. Mrs Butler, Anna, emigrated to America.
She lived with an aunt in New Jersey for six months
and then went to Los Angeles, where she works in the
office of a large insurance company — '

He breaks off because he is aware that the place is not empty. Then he sees ANNA.

Oh, you're still here. Heavens, I thought I was alone for a minute. Just the two of us. Not much point in continuing, is there?

ANNA Yes — go on. Please go on.

SIR With this?

ANNA Please.

SIR There's only — what? — two or three lines left.

ANNA Even so.

SIR 'She shares an apartment with an English girl and they go on holidays together. She owns a car and is thinking of buying an apartment of her own. She has never returned to Ireland.' And that's it.

ANNA That's all?

SIR That's all I've got here.

ANNA Are you sure?

SIR Blank pages.

ANNA I see.

She gets up and begins to move off.

SIR Did you expect there'd be something more?

ANNA I just wondered — that's all.

SIR Is there something missing?

ANNA No. Not a thing. Not a single thing.

SIR Ah. Good. Good. All right, Anna?

But she has gone. He shrugs his shoulders and closes the book. He takes a last look round the set and begins to leave. As he leaves, bring down the lights.